Pink Pages

written by Sarah Delmege

illustrated by Rachel Powell

Scholastic Inc.

New York Toronto London Auckland Sydney
Mexico City New Delhi Hong Kong Buenos Aires

Published as *My Perfect Pink Book* in the United Kingdom in 2004 by The Chicken House,
2 Palmer Street, Frome, Somerset, BA 11 1DS.

ISBN 0-439-67992-3

ISBN 13: 978-0-439-67992-3

Text by Sarah Delmege

Illustrations by Rachel Powell

Designed by Robert Elaine Wilkinson

With thanks to Margaret Histed and Veronica Weallans

First Scholastic printing, November 2004

Reprinted by Scholastic India Pvt. Ltd.,

January; July; September 2005; March; September 2006

January; June; August; November 2007; January; June; July; November 2008

January ; May ; September 2009

Printed at Kriti, New Delhi.

CONTENTS

Hi

Congratulations on picking the pinkest, most perfect book around. It's what EVERY girl should have this season – it makes boredom So last year! And it's packed with everything and anything that you'll be interested in.

Want to find out how to leap effortlessly from confusion to confidence? check out the Attitude chapter. There's a whole section on Style to make sure you always look gorgeous from head to toe. And you simply MUST read the Friendship chapter. Then find out what your future holds, in the not-to-be-missed Destiny chapter...and if it's something TOTALLY embarrassing, find out how to deal with it in the Oops chapter. If that isn't enough, then the Help chapter is crammed full of must-have tips and advice. But the best thing about this book (even if I do say so myself) is that you can either read it from cover to cover or skip around and read whatever catches your eye. It's your own personal directory of everything that's cool. So snuggle up, get comfy, and get reading.

Love, Sarah xx

ATTITUDE

How to get it, keep it,
and improve it!

8

What is the secret of

ATTITUDE POWER?

Attitude is all about confidence. It's about charming all kinds of people, from your own parents and teachers to your best friend. It's about charisma, using your powers of communication, and making connections!

Test yourself to discover your confidence level.

START

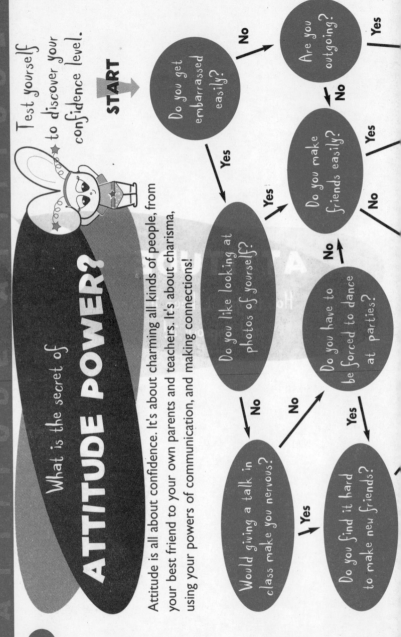

Do you get embarrassed easily?

No → Are you outgoing?

Yes

Yes ↓

Do you like looking at photos of yourself?

Yes → Do you make friends easily?

No

No

Would giving a talk in class make you nervous?

Yes ↓

Do you have to be forced to dance at parties?

Yes

No

Do you find it hard to make new friends?

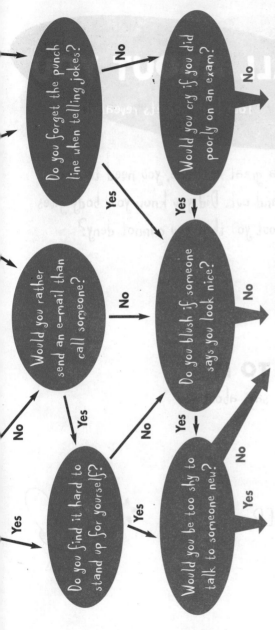

Do you forget the punch line when telling jokes?

No →

Would you rather send an e-mail than call someone?

No →

Do you find it hard to stand up for yourself?

Yes

Would you cry if you did poorly on an exam?

No →

Do you blush if someone says you look nice?

Yes

Would you be too shy to talk to someone new?

Yes

Yes

Yes

No

No

CHILLED-OUT CHICK

You're the Queen of Attitude. You take things in stride, never get flustered, and always say the right thing. Lucky you!

ATTITUDE CONTROL

Some things make you blush. At other times, you can be as cool as a cucumber. Work on keeping calm — a big smile will get you through.

BLUSH BABY

The slightest thing can make you blush. Don't worry, though, because everyone thinks you're sweet. All you have to do is laugh off those blushes!

ALL ABOUT YOU

Your body secrets revealed

To really have a great attitude, you need to know yourself inside and out. Did you know your body gives away secrets about you that you cannot deny?

FACE UP TO IT
What your face says about you

Face readers believe the shape of your face explains how you relate to others. So it's not just your smile that makes people want to meet you, it's your chin, too! Find the shape closest to yours, then read what it all means.

THE DREAMER

SHAPE: Widest at the forehead.

WHAT YOU ARE LIKE: You're passionate about what you do.

AT HOME: You're two steps ahead of your family.

WITH FRIENDS: Your superactive pals share your energy.

THE LEADER
SHAPE: Round, widest at the cheeks.
WHAT YOU ARE LIKE: Social butterfly. **AT HOME:** You are the model daughter, always excelling. **WITH FRIENDS:** You ooze confidence. Friends respect you.

THE GIVER
SHAPE: Widest at the jaw. **WHAT YOU ARE LIKE:** Could you be any nicer? No! **AT HOME:** You're the peacemaker who calms situations. **WITH FRIENDS:** You'll always go the extra mile for a friend.

THE DIPLOMAT
SHAPE: Equal from forehead to jaw. **WHAT YOU ARE LIKE:** You can win anyone over, any time. **AT HOME:** You talk to your parents, so they trust you. **WITH FRIENDS:** You make your pals feel great.

THE SURVIVOR
SHAPE: Diamond, widest at the cheekbones.
WHAT YOU ARE LIKE: Nothing is out of your reach. **AT HOME:** You deal with your problems on your own. **WITH FRIENDS:** You prefer a few deep friendships.

WHY DON'T YOU . . .
Get Interested?

How much do you really know about your mom? She had a life before you came along, so ask her about the most outrageous thing she's ever done. She may surprise you!

TOE THE LINE

Check your big toe for a quick personality assessment.

LONG: You love to talk!

SHORT: You're very private and can be shy.

ROUNDED: You're tactful, and quiet about your opinions.

SQUARE: You speak your mind.

HANDY HINTS

How your hands reveal your personality

1. FINGER SECTIONS
Look at your palms.

See how there are lines dividing your fingers into three sections?

Which section is the longest — the top, middle, or bottom?

TOP: You're intellectual and surround yourself with people whose brains match yours.

MIDDLE: Ka-ching! You're after financial success and have the skills to get there!

BOTTOM: You're all about enjoying life. You love to eat, have fun, and be spoiled rotten.

2. BENDY THUMBS

See how far back your thumb bends.

Does it form an arch or is it straight?

ARCH: You're spontaneous, versatile, talented, happy-go-lucky, and you adapt to change easily.

STRAIGHT: You're practical, even-tempered, careful with money, and can be depended upon.

3. TIPS TELL ALL

Look at your fingertips.

Which of these words best describes them?

WIDE: You're artsy and like to take risks, but you can be a total drama queen.

SQUARE: You plan ahead, and don't like spontaneity.

POINTED: You're vibrant and romantic, but can be lazy. You don't like to study or exercise.

ROUNDED: You're sweet and spiritual, but can sometimes be naïve.

4. MAKE A "V"

Splay out your fingers.

Which pair of fingers has the biggest space between them?

INDEX/MIDDLE: You're a natural leader.

MIDDLE/RING: You're laid-back.

PINKY/RING: You're full of confidence.

So now you know what your body says about you. Even if you disagree, you're one step closer to knowing yourself better.

13

ANIMAL MAGIC

What your favorite animals are reveals a lot about you.
Take this test to discover the animal in you.

Do you like yours cute and cuddly, running swift
and free, or just safe behind bars?

Whether you love them or hate them, certain animals are
associated with particular qualities. For this simple test,
choose three animals in order of preference.

HORSE	**DOG**	**POLAR BEAR**
DOLPHIN	**CAT**	**DEER**
LION	**MONKEY**	**SQUIRREL**
ELEPHANT	**GOAT**	**RHINO**
EAGLE	**WOLF**	**SHEEP**
MOUSE		

Now, from the list of words on the next page, select three
that you think best describe each animal. They could be
things that you admire or even dislike about them.

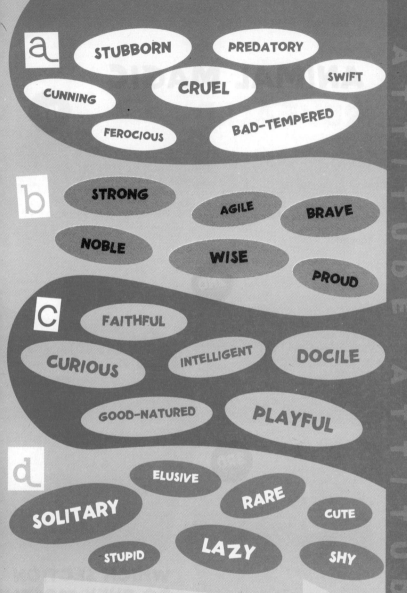

a
STUBBORN
PREDATORY
SWIFT
CUNNING
CRUEL
FEROCIOUS
BAD-TEMPERED

b
STRONG
AGILE
BRAVE
NOBLE
WISE
PROUD

c
FAITHFUL
CURIOUS
INTELLIGENT
DOCILE
GOOD-NATURED
PLAYFUL

d
ELUSIVE
RARE
SOLITARY
CUTE
STUPID
LAZY
SHY

WHAT DID YOU CHOOSE?
Turn the page to find out what it all means.

ANIMAL MAGIC REVEALED

Your choice of animals and the order you put them in should tell you a lot about yourself.

1ST
The animal you chose as your first choice is how you would like to be seen by others — it's your ideal image.

2ND
Your second choice is how others DO see you — the attitude you project.

Now let's look at the words you chose to describe each animal. This reveals more about how you see yourself and how others see you.

3RD
Your third choice is how you see yourself — how you think you really are.

WHICH SECTION DO THEY MOSTLY COME FROM?

WHY DON'T YOU . . . challenge yourself?

Make a list of ten things to achieve this week, like eating a new kind of fruit (ever heard of a guava?) or making a new friend. Make yourself do them all.

d

Do you ever come out of your shell? Your positive attitude is virtually nonexistent.

a

You beast, you! You want to be seen as mad, bad, and dangerous to know!

b

Certainly no problem with attitude here. You're positively oozing animal magnetism!

Do you need to CHANGE THAT ATTITUDE? Turn to page 32 now or take the next few tests, just to make sure . . .

c

As long as you know you can depend on someone, you'll be a loyal, steadfast friend for life.

WHICH GODDESS ARE YOU?

Take a look at the three card images.
Which one do you feel most drawn to?

There is no right or wrong answer! Just trust your
instincts here.

CARD 1 ATHENA

CARD 2 DEMETER

CARD 3
APHRODITE

If you chose: **APHRODITE**

YOU'RE THE GODDESS OF WILD

Your strengths lie in your energetic, exciting nature. The party starts with you! You embrace challenges and love new people and experiences.

If you chose: **DEMETER**

YOU'RE THE GODDESS OF COOL

Your strengths lie in your practical, down-to-earth nature. You're a trusted friend who can always be relied upon. You don't need frivolous things to make you happy. People love you because you're real.

If you chose: **ATHENA**

YOU'RE THE GODDESS OF CALM

Your strengths lie in your cautious, calm nature. You impress people by listening during conversations and then piping in with intelligent, thoughtful, or witty comments. Being quiet makes you mysterious and intriguing — don't think it's a fault!

SCHOOL RULES

Do you deal well with parents and teachers?

Parents. They can drive us crazy, but we still can't help wanting their approval. A surefire way of gaining it is to have a good attitude about school, teachers, and homework. So let's see if you'll be getting a bigger allowance — or a longer grounding — by answering these questions.

1. WHAT'S YOUR FAVORITE SUBJECT?

a Gym
b Art
c Math

2. WHICH COMMENT APPEARED MOST ON YOUR LAST REPORT CARD?

a Is very bright but doesn't...
b Tries hard, but doesn't always achieve...
c Talks too much and needs to apply herself more...

3. WHAT'S YOUR MOM OR DAD'S FAVORITE SAYING?

a "You're always daydreaming."
b "You don't ever clean up your room."
c "You're lazy."

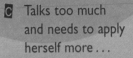

4. HOW DO YOU THINK YOU'RE DOING AT SCHOOL?
a Better than ever
b Worse than last year
c Pretty much the same as last year

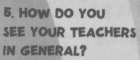

5. HOW DO YOU SEE YOUR TEACHERS IN GENERAL?
a As people who I occasionally get along with
b As people I can go to with problems
c As people from another planet

6. HAVE YOU SET GOALS FOR YOURSELF THIS YEAR?
a No, it's not something I've thought about
b A couple, but haven't done anything about them yet
c Yes, and I've fulfilled some

7. WHAT WOULD YOU LIKE MOST IN THE NEXT YEAR?
a More interests
b More friends
c To do well at school

8. HOW MUCH DO YOU TELL YOUR PARENTS ABOUT YOUR LIFE?
a Very little
b A lot, but not all
c Everything

9. HOW WOULD YOU DESCRIBE YOUR GROUP OF FRIENDS?
a A mixture — some just want to have fun, others are more serious
b Mature and hard-working
c Up for a good time

10. WHERE DO YOU SEE YOURSELF IN TEN YEARS?
a Working in a job that pays well
b In college
c No idea whatsoever

NOW TURN THE PAGE TO ADD UP YOUR SCORE.

ANSWERS

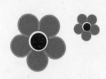

1. a 1, b 5, c 10
2. a 5, b 10, c 1
3. a 10, b 5, c 1
4. a 10, b 1, c 5
5. a 5, b 10, c 1

6. a 1, b 5, c 10
7. a 5, b 1, c 10
8. a 1, b 5, c 10
9. a 5, b 10, c 1
10. a 5, b 10, c 1

WHAT YOUR SCORE MEANS

51-100

Your parents will be singing your praises to everyone — even the mailman! You're a person who not only needs your parents' approval but actually gets it because you've got a great attitude toward school and schoolwork. That doesn't mean you can't have lots of fun, too — it's all a matter of balance. Make sure you don't always do things just to please your family. You have to go with what you want in life, not what other people want for you.

25-50

Your attitude is pretty positive, but there's room for improvement, in your parents' minds. If they start being hard on you, it's just them hoping to motivate you. If you pay attention and try harder, they will be happy with that. But moms and dads don't expect miracles, so you don't need to wear yourself out trying to be Superchild. All they want from you is your best. If you put more effort into schoolwork, friendships, and hobbies, they'll soon be embarrassing you with "my daughter is so great" stories.

24 and under

You're probably sick of hearing comments like "Why can't you be more like . . . ?" Your mom and dad are letting off steam because they can see you're not making an effort. Don't get upset and feel like you're useless. Instead, think about whether it's your attitude that's the problem or if you really have been trying hard. If it's your attitude, you know there's more you could do. But if your efforts have gone unnoticed, don't give up. Ask for help — from your parents, your teachers, or your friends. The more you achieve, the better you'll feel about yourself and the more praise you'll get.

24

A JOURNEY INTO YOUR MIND

You are going on a journey into your own mind. Write down the answers to the questions quickly; don't think about them for too long. Say whatever comes into your mind first. And no peeking ahead — you'll spoil all the fun!

START

Imagine yourself walking along a path. The path splits. Which way do you go?

a Up over the open plains.

b Down to the wooded valley.

You come across a bear.

What kind of bear is it?

There is a
stick nearby.

What kind of
stick is it?

Do you
pick it up?

Yes.

No.

If yes,
why?

a

To lean on.

b

For self-defense.

You walk on a
little farther and
come to water.

Describe what
you see.

Beyond
the water
is land.

What kind
of water is it?

Now turn
the page
to find out
what it all
means.

25

EXPLANATION

THE PATH TAKEN

This represents your attitude toward life. **THE OPEN PLAINS** show a willingness to take risks. You are open to new ideas and experiences. **THE WOODED VALLEY** suggests that you prefer to feel sheltered and protected.

THE BEAR

This represents how you see other people. Do you see them as threatening (a great big grizzly bear) or friendly and approachable (a cute teddy bear)?

THE STICK

This represents how you deal with other people. Did you pick up the stick? **YES** means that you are defensive. If **NO**, you meet people openly. Your purpose for the stick shows how you feel about your opinions. **FOR SELF-DEFENSE** means you're prepared to fight against other people's ideas if they don't agree with yours.

TO LEAN ON means you're comfortable with your opinions.

THE WATER

This represents how you would like your life to be. Is it a stream — cool, refreshing, and lively — or a calm sea, inviting you to dip your toes in it? Is it a raging rapid, exciting and dangerous? Or is it a muddy pond that's flat and safe but dull?

THE LAND AHEAD

This represents your attitude about the future. Is it a fruitful, flowering land, full of promise and adventure? Is it a barren wasteland? Or do you see difficult mountains to climb?

BY NOW YOU'VE HAD A GOOD LOOK AT YOUR ATTITUDE.

You've probably started thinking about how your attitude affects you, your friends, your family, and your life. After reading this chapter, you may feel really positive — you may even feel like getting out there and conquering the world!

REMEMBER

YOU CAN DO ANYTHING!

We can all get what we want out of life, just not always in the order we want it. With the right attitude, one thing is sure: The future is going to be really exciting, and it's all yours. Go for it!

Super!

BE POSITIVE!

Now you should have a clearer idea about the kind of attitude you have. But there's one really important thing to keep in mind.

IMPORTANT RULE TO BE FOLLOWED AT ALL TIMES

Don't ever try to be someone you're not. People will see through you right away. To have the best attitude, be true to yourself.

That's right, the secret to having a great attitude is to be yourself and be happy with who you are. It doesn't matter what you look like or where your strengths lie.

Do you remember that Christina Aguilera song? The one that goes, *"I am beautiful, no matter what they say"*? Well, our Christina may not always be number one in fashion, but when it comes to attitude, she's right on.

TIPS FOR FEELING GOOD ABOUT YOURSELF... ALWAYS!

- Care less about what other people think.
- Do things or wear things that make YOU happy.
- Value your friends and family and they will value you.
- Look at the good things in your life. Look at the good things in you.

28

The more we recognize our greatness, the more wonderful we become. Obviously, you don't want to get carried away and get a swelled head, but you don't have to be an arrogant show-off to feel good about yourself.

So next time you're feeling down on yourself, stop and think about it. What would you prefer to hear one of your friends say?

a

I failed all my tests. I'm in a fight with my boyfriend, and I'm ugly.

b

I'm doing well in school, and I've got the best friends anyone could ever have.

Clue: The answer here should be B. (If you answered A, please turn to page 32 immediately!)

People who have a great attitude know what they like about themselves. They aren't constantly down on everything they do. They choose to look at what's good rather than what's bad.

Get a clean sheet of paper and at the top write:

"I am great because . . ."

Then make a list of all the reasons you ARE great. (No modesty here, please. Reach inside yourself and drag out those good qualities.)

Now, if you get an attack of self-doubt, look at yourself in the mirror and recite that list. You may feel a little wacky doing it, but the more you say it, the more you'll believe it. Before long, you're going to have the best attitude in town.

Every girl's surefire tips to a

GREAT ATTITUDE!

1. EYE CONTACT Get it, maintain it, and use it.

2. ACT CONFIDENT AND CAPABLE Everyone likes people who like themselves. So quit the *"I'm hopeless at EVERYTHING"* stuff. It's not pretty!

3. BE YOURSELF Just go your own way. Being natural is far better than faking it and feeling uneasy.

4. HAVE CONVERSATION TOPICS You don't need to walk around with a checklist, but remember to start conversations by bringing up something easy to talk about — like a TV show or a rock group.

5. BE HAPPY Sparkling eyes and a smile that can light up a room . . . you can't go wrong. And this is true even if you've got braces!

6. DANCE MOVES Having attitude is as much about the way you move as the way you look and act, which is why dance floors are the ideal place to impress. Worried about your moves? Try to have fun and don't take yourself too seriously. Check out MTV for inspiration — for the ultimate in attitude, Beyoncé has got it going on!

7. DITCH THE DIVA

Do you throw tantrums? Are you super-demanding while doing little in return? Don't let the diva in you take over. And if she does, be ready to make some serious apologies.

8. MAKE A PLAN

Aim to make the best of what you've got or make a plan to get what you want. Save your money so you can afford that new pair of jeans. You really can have what you want; you just have to believe in yourself and work hard toward your goals.

9. USE PEOPLE'S NAMES

a lot. If you've just met, using people's names shows them you can remember who they are. It will make them feel important and wanted.

10. COMMUNICATE

Open up about yourself, giving someone even more reason to like you. But don't go on and on — the goal is to make people feel both interested and interesting, not to bore them to death.

Want to know more about someone? Watch them eat. New research says that the way a person holds their fork and knife reveals their personality.

DAINTY (FORK PRONGS DOWN)
Cautious, thoughtful, conformist
PEN (HOLDS KNIFE LIKE A PEN) Practical, not much imagination, but good at details
STABBER (FORK ONLY)
Spontaneous, but short attention span
SHOVEL (FORK PRONGS UP)
Easygoing, fun-loving, and open, but can be lazy

31

CHANGE THAT ATTITUDE

Is your attitude going to take you far in life or does it need a makeover? If you're not sure, here's a final test.

QUIZ

Look at these lists. You are more likely to:

a Pick up litter.

b Drop litter on the street.

a Help wash the dishes.

b Stomp to your room, shouting, "I didn't ask to be born!"

a Talk to the new girl at school.

b Be nasty about the new girl at school.

a Turn in a lost purse full of cash.

b Turn in the purse but spend the cash.

ANSWER

IF YOU ANSWERED MOSTLY As, YOU'RE WELL ON YOUR WAY TO HAVING A GREAT ATTITUDE.

If you answered mostly Bs, you've got work to do. Maybe you've done bad things in the past — being cruel, lying, cheating, or even stealing — but it doesn't mean that's all you're capable of. You can drop the loser attitude any time you like, and NOW is the time to change.

Whether your attitude toward yourself, toward life, or toward others needs work, don't worry. These things take time, and all the legwork and effort you put in now will pay off!

REMEMBER THE TORTOISE AND THE HARE? KEEP AT IT AND YOU'LL END UP A WINNER!

PEARLS OF WISDOM

When something in your life goes wrong . . .
chalk it up to experience and move on.

If the things you want are out of reach . . .
then, chances are, they wouldn't have made you happy anyway.

If that girl's hair is always perfect
and her clothes are way cooler than yours . . .
it doesn't necessarily mean she's any happier than you.

tell that inner critic
to take a hike!

STYLE

What is it
and how do you get it?

What is the secret of
STYLE?

Style is all about looking and feeling great. It's not about what everyone else is wearing. It's about self-expression. This is the 21st century and it's time to wear what you want, how you want! So what's your style? Take this test to find out.

Girly? Tomboy? Rocker chick? When it comes to your look, what are you like?

START

Do you prefer jeans to miniskirts?
— No / Yes

Do your friends admire your style?
— No / Yes

Do you prefer Britney Spears to Christina Aguilera?
— No / Yes

Does long hair look cooler than short hair?
— No / Yes

Do you take nail polish off as soon as it's chipped?
— No / Yes

Do you often wear lip gloss or glitter?

Is art one of your favorite subjects in school?

Yes

No

Do you like wearing black?

Yes

No

Is comfort more important than fashion?

No

Yes

Do you adore shopping?

Yes

No

Do you often change your hairstyle and accessories?

No

Yes

Do you usually carry a mirror everywhere?

Yes

No

Do you love glossy magazines?

Yes

GIRLY

You're a girly girl who loves clothes, makeup, and accessories. You like to look neat and pretty, and you wouldn't dream of going out looking anything less than perfect.

INDIVIDUAL

You're artsy and love experimenting with wild new looks! You hate following the crowd, preferring to stand out and turn heads with your unique style.

TOMBOY

Beauty supplies and makeup are low on your list. You feel that life is too short to be stuck in your room painting your nails. You'd rather be out having fun.

37

WHAT DOES YOUR LOOK SAY ABOUT YOU?

Is your day one long search for a mirror? It's confession time.

THE QUIZ

Oh, no! You've slept through your alarm (again) and you're running late to go shopping with your mom. But before you rush out the front door, you take one final look in the mirror to check that:

 Your hair looks good.

 You don't have any crumbs stuck between your teeth.

 Your lip gloss is perfectly in place.

You're not exactly thrilled with what you see. What do you do about it?

 Dash back to your bedroom to carefully reapply your lip gloss and hair accessories.

 Run your fingers through your hair.

 Stick your tongue out at your reflection and dash out.

38

In the car, you pull out a magazine to catch up on all the gossip. Studying a picture of Britney, you decide:

 She really is talented.

 She might look better with a more natural look.

 She needs a new stylist and she needs one NOW.

You arrive at the mall and you and your mom get out of the car. In the parking lot, it starts raining. You immediately:

 Pop under an awning.

 Laugh it off.

 Run to the nearest bathroom to check that you still look gorgeous.

At last, you're inside! At the makeup counter, you:

 Know exactly what you need and throw it all into your basket.

 Buy a new shade of lip gloss.

 Look at a few things but don't buy anything new.

Then it's straight on to your favorite clothes store. As soon as you walk in the door, you:

 Try on everything — you want to look good for tonight's party.

 Buy whatever Mom says looks best.

 Head straight for the accessories. You've already bought the perfect outfit for tonight.

Arriving at the party that night, you head straight for the dance floor. While shaking your stuff, you notice some girls looking in your direction. You:

 Glance behind you to make sure your skirt isn't tucked into your underwear.

 Smile and look away.

 Grin in their direction and do more of your best moves for them to admire.

You go to the bathroom. As you're washing your hands, you inspect your face in the mirror. You see your hair is looking a little messy. You:

 Forget about it and go back to your friends.

 Try to fluff it back up and not stress out.

 Get out your brush and groom it back to perfection.

It's time to leave. When you get home, you can't stop yawning, so you:

 Head to the bathroom to wash your face, brush your teeth, and put on moisturizer.

 Wash and brush as always, but very quickly.

 Immediately fall into bed and crash.

THE RESULTS

Which symbol did you choose the most?

MOSTLY STARS
GLAM GIRL

You're addicted to looking good at all costs. But being hooked on beauty can eat up a whole lot of time and money. Imagine what you could accomplish if you channeled some of that energy into school, sports, or having fun! Remember, beauty is only skin deep, and we know you're soooo much deeper than that!

MOSTLY SHOES
NATURAL BEAUTY

You're prepared to go just the right distance for beauty. Although a great hairstyle or lip gloss can really perk up your weekend, you wouldn't have a major stress-out if you were having a bad hair day. You know your identity is about who you are and not what shade of glitter you're wearing.

MOSTLY LIPS
PLAIN JANE

It's great that you're low-key about your looks. But you should get past the idea that caring about your looks is shallow. It's not — it just means that you want the outer you to reflect who you are inside. So even if you'd rather go low-maintenance, don't be shy about learning a few beauty tricks. Knowing how to make the best of what you've got is a real confidence booster that can make you feel great.

TOP TEN STYLE TIPS

bows

buttons

patches

shoes

1 Everyone can be stylish. You don't have to be outgoing, rich, or beautiful. Style is not about bold statements and expensive fashions; it's about being creative and knowing what goes well together and what looks good on you.

2 Make an effort. Think about what you like and the look you want to achieve.

3 Don't scrimp on the things you love to wear. If you wear jeans all the time, or love great-looking shoes, buy what really suits you and you'll never regret it. Save money on the less important things.

4 Experiment. Go to different shops and try on clothes and colors that you don't normally wear. If you're not sure they look good on you, take a friend along for a second opinion.

5 **Accessorize. A bag, a hat, or a necklace can add a dash of style to the dullest of outfits. Even a hair clip can brighten up your look.**

6 Don't wear anything that isn't comfortable. If you don't feel good, you won't look good — it's as simple as that.

7 Never wear clothes that are too small for you. They won't make you look slimmer — just the opposite!

8 Make the most of what you've got. If you're short on cash and bored with your clothes, take time to make up new outfits. Pull two random items out of your closet and put them on. You might come up with a great new look — and you'll have fun doing it!

9 Customize. Think creatively about how you can jazz up your clothes to make them uniquely you. Dyes, patches, buttons, and bows can be a cheap way to super-styledom.

10 Pick a role model or style icon — a celeb, a singer, even a big sister! Notice what they wear — what style of jeans, what kind of accessories — then re-create the look to suit you.

CRAZY ABOUT COLOR

Did you know the colors you wear can actually change your mood? Read on to find out how.

BLACK IS BACK Slipping into something black can give you that I-know-what-I-want-and-I'm-going-to-get-it kind of feeling. If you're tired of going along with the crowd, wear black and watch people sit up and take notice.

THINK PINK Looking pretty in pink will make you feel grrrreat and others will take an instant liking to you. Put on something pink and you'll have lots of admirers.

FEELING BLUE Blue oozes calm and is the color of truth. So if you think a friend's not being honest with you, grab something blue from your wardrobe, settle down for a heart-to-heart, and watch as she suddenly opens up.

SERENE GREEN If you have a big decision to make, or if something is worrying you, then green's the color to wear. It helps you feel decisive and clearheaded and it really gets those creative juices flowing.

PERFECT PURPLE When you feel like you got up on the wrong side of the bed or have no energy, simply reach for purple. Wearing the color purple will have you feeling full of energy and back to your normal self.

But which colors best fit you? It all depends on your hair color, skin tone — and attitude. Below is a general guide, but the best way to tell what's best for you is to try on different colors and get opinions from trusted friends.

PINK SKIN, BLOND OR FAIR HAIR Chocolate brown, pale olive, bright green, pale blue, powder blue, all shades of pink, and most shades of purple.

PALE SKIN, RED HAIR All greens, pastel blues, purples and pinks, denim colors, black and gray.

MEDIUM SKIN, BROWN HAIR Black, dark denim, gray, bright red, blue-greens and green-blues, white, and blue-purples.

OLIVE SKIN, BROWN OR BLACK HAIR All reds and browns, white, violet, bright blues, and muted pinks.

BROWN SKIN, DARK HAIR Most reds, especially orange-red, white, soft blues, purples and pinks, neon greens and yellows, purple, and violet.

SKIN WITH YELLOW UNDERTONES, DARK HAIR Dark berry reds, bright reds, black, green, pale blues, and dark purples.

Six Easy steps to funky nails

1. Tell your friends to bring all their nail polishes over.

2. Clean and file your fingernails.

3. Paint your nails. Use one color, three colors, or lots of colors! Try spots and stripes, too.

4. While the nail polish is still wet, dip your nails in glitter to add a special sparkle.

5. When your nails are dry, put on a layer of clear nail polish to seal the glitter.

Show off your fab designs.

45

1

START →

The mall is your second home.

YES Forward 1
NO Forward 2

2
You drool over a gorgeous top. Do you buy it without even thinking?

YES Forward 6
NO Forward 2

3
Your dressing room ends up covered in clothes that you don't often buy.

YES Forward 2
NO Forward 3

4
You love nothing better than finding a bargain.

YES Forward
NO Forward 1

14
You enjoy going shopping even when you have no money to spend.

YES Forward 3
NO Forward 1

13
The thought of shopping makes you tingle with joy.

YES Forward 1
NO Forward 3

12 TRY THIS ON FOR SIZE

You're SUCH a bargain hunter. Your purse is only pried open if there's a bargain involved. But before you buy, ask yourself, "Do I *really* want this?" Pass up a few of those amazing but useless deals and you'll have the cash for the things you REALLY want

15
You prefer to buy from catalogues because it's less hassle.

YES Forward 2
NO Forward 4

WHAT'S YOUR SHOPPING STYLE?

Play this game to find out.

25
You find something you like. Do you shop around for the best price?

YES Go to 12
NO Back 2

24
You always think about what you've got to go with an item before you buy it.

YES Go to 7
NO Back 6

23 TRY THIS ON FOR SIZE

To you, shopping is a drag. You've go better things to do than scour sales ra and don't care that your jeans are tw years old. Next time you're dragged o shopping, why not try different thing on? Just for fun!

5 You look at magazines for current fashion tips before you buy anything.

YES Forward 3
NO Forward 5

6 You like to shop armed with a list of what you need.

YES Forward 3
NO Back 1

7 TRY THIS ON FOR SIZE

You know what's hip and what to skip. You take time to get the scoop on new styles and do a wardrobe check before buying things you don't need. You're no slave to fashion — when you buy, you buy what suits you. You do splurge on special things — if they are too good to resist.

11 You find a fab T-shirt at a rock-bottom price. Do you buy one in every color?

YES Forward 1
NO Back 5

10 You'd rather spend time buying CDs than buying clothes.

YES Forward 4
NO Back 1

9 You buy a gorgeous skirt at half price. Do you brag about your bargain?

YES Forward 6
NO Forward 4

8 You love the latest fashion but it doesn't really suit you. Do you buy, anyway?

YES Forward 5
NO Forward 6

16 You try on jeans that are to die for but have two similar pairs at home. Do you buy?

YES Forward 4
NO Forward 5

17 You often say "If I don't like it I can take it back" but rarely do.

YES Forward 2
NO Back 1

18 TRY THIS ON FOR SIZE

It's practically impossible for you to shop without buying. You've got so many clothes, they don't all fit in your closet and your fashion magazines are piled high. Maybe it's time to ask yourself if you actually need everything you buy.

22 When you get a fab new pair of shoes, you wear them until they fall apart.

YES Forward 1
NO Forward 3

21 You find the dress of your dreams but don't have the money. Do you borrow?

YES Forward 3
NO Forward 4

20 Lining up to buy a sweater, you spot a skirt and purse to match. Do you buy them all?

YES Forward 4
NO Forward 1

19 Every occasion is an excuse to shop for a new outfit.

YES Back 1
NO Forward 3

JAZZ UP YOUR WARDROBE

Want to make a great new purse? Instead of throwing away your old, worn-out clothes, cut them up into patchwork squares. Then check the purses in thrift stores to find one made of fabric. Pin your squares onto the fabric purse randomly so the patterns are varied, and sew around the edges using simple stitches such as cross-stitch or zigzag. Use a different brightly colored thread for each square so it really stands out against the fabric. Patchwork paradise!

Want to make over an old purse?
Simply cut out the back pockets of an old pair of jeans and sew one pocket on to either side of the purse. A perfect place for your lip gloss! And you can always use an old belt to make a funky strap.

If you want to liven up a pair of boring pants, get some lace or any trimming you like, unpick the side seam of each leg, and sew in the lace. Simple, but oh, so effective! (Don't forget to ask your mom if it's OK!)

To instantly transform an outfit . . . All you have to do is add a glam choker or a necklace. Voilà! Instant fabulous!

If you have an old pair of jeans that have become too short, just cut off the bottoms to make them into capris! You could also cut off the waistband so they have a ripped effect at the top!

You can make a funky wristband by simply raiding your sock drawer! Argyle socks are great for this, but you can use any kind. Cut off the foot of the sock and the elasticized top so you're left with a tube. Simply fold a three-quarter-inch seam inside each end of the tube to disguise the raw edges and sew the seams down. Turn it around the right way and wear it with attitude!

To make old sneakers more interesting, get yourself a stencil kit and a permanent marker. Pick a word or saying you like. Hold the stencil in place and carefully write each letter.

Tip: Have some tissue handy so you can wipe off any mistakes before they dry. And voilà! A cool pair of 100% original sneakers!

To make your eyelashes sparkle . . . Put glitter gel on a clean toothbrush and gently brush the gel onto your lashes.

49

FRUITY BEAUTY

Here are some great recipes for a truly scrumptious pampering session, coming soon to a sleepover near you.

FEED YOUR FACE

EYE EYE!

Three ways to keep your peepers in top condition.

1 Place cool cucumber slices over your eyelids and relax for about twenty minutes. The cucumber will make your eyes feel really cool and fresh, and will get rid of puffiness.

2 Lie back and relax for about fifteen minutes with two cold, damp teabags over your eyes. This is especially good if you feel or look tired, because it reduces any dark circles under your eyes, leaving you looking bright-eyed.

3 Leave two teaspoons in the fridge for about an hour. Remove them, place the bulbs of the spoons over your eyes, and then rest. This is a good one for the morning after your sleepover — it really wakes you up!

Beauty experts are always telling us to eat lots of fruit and vegetables to keep our skin healthy from the inside. But did you know that feeding your skin from the outside will also keep it glowing with health? You can buy face masks in any drugstore, or you can make your own. Below are two delicious recipes.

LAZY GIRL MASK

ALL YOU NEED:
three strawberries and a kiwi

WHAT TO DO:
1. Slice up the strawberries and kiwi.
2. Put the slices directly onto your face and relax. (Now you see how this one got its name!)

MAGIC MASK RECIPE

ALL YOU NEED:
one ripe avocado and a teaspoon of honey

WHAT TO DO:
1. Peel the avocado and remove the pit.
2. Mash up the avocado in a bowl with the honey.
3. Apply to your face smoothly and evenly. Then relax.

HOW TO USE A MASK

1 Tie your hair back from your face.

2 Clean your face gently using a cleansing lotion or mild soap and water.

3 Apply the mask lightly with your fingertips, avoiding the eye and mouth areas. Make sure you put it on smoothly, right up to your hairline.

4 Lie down and relax for five to ten minutes.

5 Rinse the mask off gently with lukewarm water (some masks peel off) and pat your skin dry with a towel.

6 Put on some moisturizer and admire your glowing skin.

51

HAIR RECIPES

Here are recipes for a do-it-yourself shampoo and a gorgeously rich conditioner. No chemicals, no perfumes, just natural goodness.

EGG-CELLENT SHAMPOO

ALL YOU NEED:
One egg (two for long hair)

WHAT TO DO:
1. Beat the egg(s) in a mixing bowl.
2. Massage the mixture into your dry hair and leave for five minutes.
3. Rinse your hair thoroughly in cool water.
4. Condition and style as normal (or use the mayonnaise recipe below).

MAYONNAISE CONDITIONER

ALL YOU NEED:
A jar of mayonnaise

WHAT TO DO:
1. Smooth a good dollop of mayonnaise onto wet hair.
2. Leave it on for five minutes, then rinse out.
3. Dry your hair and — voilà! — you have a beautiful, vibrant mane. Hellooo, gorgeous!

LUSCIOUS LIPS

Make your own lip balm.

ALL YOU NEED:
Vaseline, different shades of lipstick, and a small container (an empty lip balm container is perfect!)

WHAT TO DO:
1. Put a large blob of Vaseline on your hand, then mix in the lipstick.
2. Keep adding color until you've found a color you like and the mixture is nice and soft.
3. Scoop the mixture off your hand into the container. Presto — instant lip balm! (Plus, no one else in the entire world will have the exact same shade as you!)

AND LAST BUT NOT LEAST...

An easy way to get great-smelling feet is to mash up two bananas with two tablespoons of sugar. Gradually stir in a cup of warm milk (get an adult's help to warm the milk) until you have a smooth, thick mixture. Rub on your feet as you would moisturizer. After three minutes, rinse your feet with warm water and dry them. You can then paint your toenails and you'll have not only gorgeous-looking but gorgeous-smelling feet!

HAIR STYLE

Love your hair

Tired of having the same old hair, day in and day out? Try these ideas and you'll never be bored with your hair again.

1 Check out hairstyles you like in magazines and try out at least two of the ideas.

2 Tie up a section of your hair at the roots with a narrow ribbon tied in a knot. The ends of the ribbon should reach the tips of your hair. Braid the ribbon into the hair for a splash of color.

3 Try a hair wrap. Experiment with a cool scarf tied in various ways, either as a headband, around a ponytail, or as a complete head wrap.

4 Create some tiny braids. Take just a few strands of hair and braid them from the roots to the ends. Leave the rest of your hair straight.

5 Tuck your hair behind your ears. If you usually wear it that way, try wearing it in front of your ears.

6 Buy a hair accessory. Get a giant barrette or silk flower and clip it in for instant glamor.

7 Slick it all back. This works for any hair length. Comb gel through with a fine-tooth comb and let your hair dry naturally.

8 Ask a pal to play stylist. She styles your hair and you style hers. Get creative!

54

9 Change your part. If you have a center part, move it to the side. If you wear a side part, move it to the center or the opposite side. Or you could try a zigzag part.

10 Add some extensions. You can buy hairpieces in a beauty supply store. Try clipping on a fake ponytail if your hair is long enough to tie back. If your hair is short, you can add clip-on pieces underneath.

WHAT YOUR HAIR SAYS ABOUT YOU

Think it's just something that grows out of your head? Think again. How you wear your hair speaks volumes.

SHORT HAIR
You're fun-loving and an inspiration to others. You find it hard to hide your emotions and want to be surrounded by happiness.

MEDIUM-LENGTH HAIR
You're a friendly gal and expect honesty from your friends. You're also easily bored and need to be busy.

LONG HAIR
You love all things girly. You like to surprise your friends and don't like to follow the crowd.

FIVE STEPS TO GORGEOUS, SHINY HAIR

1 Wash your hair with a gentle shampoo.

2 Comb some conditioner through, leave in for a minute, then rinse your hair.

3 Gently towel it dry.

4 Now style your hair. Try using hot curlers to make your hair wavy. Or if your hair's wavy, why not try straighteners for a different look?

5 Put some anti-frizz gel or mousse on your hair for that extra bit of shine!

PEARLS OF WISDOM

Keep your legs uncrossed and sit up straight at the hairdresser's or you could end up with an uneven cut.

Fashion is something you buy. Style is something you have.

Style is not just about looking good. It's also about feeling good.

Most models' careers are over by the time they're 23!

Protect your skin! ALWAYS WEAR SUNSCREEN!

FRIENDS

Where would we be
without them?

Super!

FRIENDS

FRIENDSHIP

Don't ya just love it?

Where would we be without our friends?
Miserable and lonely, that's where.

Most girls know there is nothing better than hanging out with our best galpals. Friends boost our self-esteem and teach us about ourselves. They help us get a grip on what is important in life — whether it's fun, loyalty, or honesty.

TEN REASONS WHY FRIENDS ROCK!

1 They still love you even when you embarrass yourself in public.

2 You've got someone to share your secrets with.

3 You've always got a shoulder to cry on.

4 Best pals always come to your parties and sleepovers.

5 They're used to your snoring, so they don't complain.

6 You've always got someone to talk things over with.

7 They can make you giggle just by looking at you.

8 You can borrow each other's stuff.

9 They're always around for a good makeover session.

10 They understand when you're having a bad day.

YOU KNOW YOU'VE GOT A BEST FRIEND WHEN...

You don't know how you ever managed without each other!

You know what she's going to say before she says it.

People start getting your names confused.

Your bedrooms look exactly the same.

Her mom introduces you as one of the family.

You can't remember which CDs are yours and which are hers.

Your phone bill has doubled since you met her.

The sidewalk between your houses is worn down.

You know her whole wardrobe by heart.

You know it's her calling before you answer the phone.

You know her biggest secret, but haven't told a soul.

You know each other better than you know yourselves.

TRUE FRIENDS' CHALLENGE

How well do you know each other?

You always hang out together, but how much do you know about your best friend? Take this challenge to find out.

WHAT TO DO

Read aloud the following list of statements to your friend and get her to write down whether she thinks the statement is true or false. Then see if she's right! When you've finished, it's your friend's turn to read out the questions and for you to guess.

I've got a great singing voice.
I LOVE Justin Timberlake.
I've had the same bedroom my whole life.
I'd like to get married one day.
I once had a really embarrassing haircut.
I'm really good with my money.
I like Brussels sprouts.
I wear size four shoes.
I'm shy when meeting new people.
I'm good at sports.

RESULTS

IF YOU GOT 7 OR MORE CORRECT
You two know each other well. Keep up the good friendship!

IF YOU GOT BETWEEN 3 AND 6
You are probably new friends and you've got lots of fun ahead of you as you find out everything about each other.

IF YOU GOT LESS THAN 3
You've got a lot of talking and learning to do, but that's the best part of friendship!

Hanging out with friends can be the happiest times of our lives! A great way to remember such special times is to start a friendship file. This is an album or scrapbook where you stick photos, pictures, ticket stubs, and other memorabilia from fantastic days with your friends. By capturing the moment, you and your friends will be able to look back in years to come and laugh at the good old days.

THE DOs AND DON'Ts OF FRIENDSHIP

You can have a falling out with a friend as quickly as you can make one. But don't despair — follow these simple DOs and DON'Ts for stress-free friendships.

DO . . .

make them cards or give them presents now and again to show them how much they mean to you.

DO . . .

let your pals have their own opinions. You can always agree to disagree.

DO . . .

tell your friends if you're upset or worried. You'll feel better and your friends will understand. They'll probably be able to help, or at least make you feel better.

DON'T . . .

bombard them with cards and gifts. They'll think you're going overboard.

DON'T . . .

insist that you do everything together. Even the best of friends need space — and then you'll have more to chat about!

DON'T . . .

ever reveal a secret she's told you. If she confesses to you that she still sucks her thumb, it's not your business to go spreading it around.

DO . . .

stick up for your pals or get help if they're being teased or bullied. You'd want them to help you out if you were in trouble, wouldn't you?

DO . . .

try to make new pals even if you've got a lot already. Meeting people is lots of fun, and you might really click.

DO . . .

give your pals attention. No one likes to feel neglected. If a pal seems down, cheer her up!

DO . . .

be there for your friends whenever they need you. You know if you were upset they'd be there with tissues, chocolate, and your favorite DVD, so do the same for them.

DON'T . . .

complain constantly. Being a whiner won't help you in your friendships one bit, so listen to your friends and cheer up if they tell you to.

DON'T . . .

get jealous when your friends meet new people. You may feel neglected, but jealousy will make it worse. If they invite you along, go! If your friend likes them, chances are you will, too.

DON'T . . .

laugh at your friend if she shows up looking less stylish than your grandma. Be constructive and help her pick a new outfit that looks better on her.

DON'T . . .

laugh at your pals when they embarrass themselves. You might think it's hilarious when they drop their food in their lap, but you have to keep a straight face. Well, at least try, anyway!

63

SIX STEPS TO MAKING NEW FRIENDS

You can never have too many friends. So check out these friend-making tips, and you might just pick up a few new pals!

1. JOIN A CLUB It may sound obvious, but you won't meet any new people sitting at home in front of the TV. There are lots of ways to meet new people outside your classroom. One of the best ways is to join an after-school club. This doesn't mean you have to sign up for extra math every week or a chess club (unless you like chess!). Why not join a singing or drama club or even a karate club at your local sports center? You'll meet a whole bunch of people in no time!

2. WHO'S INTO WHAT? So you've met a few people. What do you do next? Well, you need to check out who has friendship potential. You can bet that the girl in the corner dangling another girl by her ankles isn't gonna make a great pal, so strike up a conversation with girls who look a little more friendly! Ask people what they're into. What music do they like? Do they watch your favorite TV shows? Before you know it, you could have discovered the only person in the country who likes *The Simpsons* as much as you do.

3. CRACK A JOKE What's essential in any good pal? A sense of humor, of course! So test any new people you meet by telling them your funniest, most gut-splitting joke and seeing if they laugh. Or try telling them the story of how you licked the icing off all the cakes at the school bake sale. If they laugh and tell you a story of their own, then you could be on the way to a new friendship.

4. TELL A SECRET

A great way to make someone feel like they're a real friend is to let them in on a secret. It doesn't have to be anything major, just some good gossip that you haven't told anyone yet! Once you've swapped secrets, compared favorite singers, and told each other your embarrassing stories, then you definitely count as friends.

5. BE INTERESTED

Half the fun of making a new friend is finding out about them. So don't spend all of the time telling them about what you like doing and what your favorite things are. Ask them questions, and you'll get along much better. Don't be afraid to disagree. Lots of friendships start off with a good, heated debate.

6. MEET AND GREET

The main, unbreakable rule when you make a new pal is to not neglect your old ones! You don't want to lose any of them because you're spending all your time with your new friend. Instead, get together as a group. When you're having a sleepover or going shopping, invite your new pal along to meet your old friends. Before you know it, everyone will know one another, and you'll have a new member in your group. Mission accomplished!

How to make lots of friends in just one week

MONDAY	Smile at everyone who looks at you.
TUESDAY	Ask a favor of someone.
WEDNESDAY	Do something nice for someone (not current friends or family).
THURSDAY	Organize a sleepover.
FRIDAY	Talk to someone at school you've never spoken to before.
SATURDAY	Go somewhere you've never been before.
SUNDAY	Call a person you know and like but don't keep in touch with.

Three tricks when speaking to others

1 Be nice first, instead of waiting to see if others will be nice to you.

2 If you don't know what to say, listen.

3 Remember, everyone likes to talk about themselves, so ask questions.

A RECIPE FOR FRIENDSHIP

INGREDIENTS

An extra large helping of confidence

·

A relaxed attitude

·

A smile

·

Things to do and talk about

·

A huge helping of curiosity and interest

METHOD

1. Combine all the above ingredients and mix well. Bring slowly to a boil and leave to simmer.

2. Garnish with a sprinkling of humor and laughter, and mix well. Voilà, the most irresistibly friendly combination ever!

TROUBLESHOOTING

This is a very simple recipe to follow, but don't despair if your friendship boils over occasionally, burns, or even goes a little stale. This is perfectly normal. Just mix up all of the ingredients again and start from the beginning.

FRIENDSHIP CHECKLIST

Think friendly ✓
Act friendly ✓
Look friendly ✓
Be friendly ✓

SLEEPOVER MAKEOVER

Tips for a perfect night

step 1 Get Mom and/or Dad on your side

Even if you're having only a small sleepover, you still must ask for permission first. Choose your moment carefully — you'll get nowhere if you hassle your mom while she's making dinner or watching her favorite TV show. Wait until the person you want to ask has time to listen.

step 2 Be prepared

Make a list of the people you want to invite and stick to it! Don't be pushed into asking people you don't know or like just because you think it'll make you more popular. Hand out invitations to show you really mean business. Get everyone to bring their makeup and accessories.

A QUICK TIP :

Before the sleepover, remove all the breakables from your room and put them in another room where they'll be safe. For an extra-special touch, tie a couple of balloons to your door and hang some string lights.

step 3 Food fun

1 Sandwiches, pizza, chips, and other small, simple snacks are the perfect sleepover food. And you can't go wrong with ice cream.

2 Fussy friends can be difficult to feed! Get around it by suggesting that everyone bring their favorite food — whether it's a big tub of popcorn or cheese and crackers.

3 If your parents are worried about spills, avoid dark juices or sodas. Make your own punch with lemonade and pieces of fruit.

step 4 Makeover mayhem

You'll need: lots of makeup, clothes, nail polish remover, copies of magazines for fashion and beauty tips — and your *Pink Pages*, of course, to look at while you're waiting to be made over.

step 5 Clean up

Once all your guests have gone home, it's time to clear away all the half-eaten cookies and empty soda cans. It can be a long, messy, and boring task, but don't leave it to your mom and dad. Cleaning up after yourself shows responsibility, and if you do a good job, your parents will be less likely to say no to your next makeover party. Hurray!

TRUTH OR DARE

A game of honesty

Just how honest are you with your friends?
Play this game if you feel brave enough.

WHAT YOU NEED

A pair of dice
A jar of mustard
A plate of cold baked beans
A few pairs of (clean!) pants
A plastic cup of water
A tablespoon
A tube of lipstick

HOW TO PLAY

It couldn't be easier. Each of you takes turns throwing both dice. Read the truth question that matches your score. You can choose to answer the question truthfully or to do one of the dares on the next page. If you choose to do a dare, throw both dice again to see which dare you must do.

Note: If you've already answered a question or done a dare, simply throw the dice again.

GOOD LUCK! AND REMEMBER — NO CHEATING!

YOUR SCORE

TRUTH QUESTIONS

2 What's the worst lie you've ever told?

3 What's the most stupid thing you've ever done?

4 If you were a boy for a day, what's the first thing you'd do?

5 Do you pick your nose?

6 What's the most embarrassing thing you've ever done?

7 If someone offered you $100 to tell your best friend's most secret secret, would you tell it?

8 Have you ever told a crush that you like him?

9 Have you ever lied to your parents?

10 What would people say is your worst fault?

11 What's the most embarrassing CD you own?

12 What's your favorite feature of your body and why?

 FRIENDS

DARES

 2 Sing any song that your friends ask you to.

 3 Eat a tiny spoonful of mustard.

 4 Wear a pair of pants on your head until your next turn.

 5 Do a Beyoncé impression.

6 Whistle or hum your favorite song.

 7 Do a dance routine to any 'NSync song.

 8 Eat one tablespoonful of cold baked beans.

 9 Balance a plastic cup of water on the back of your hand for three seconds.

 10 Do a dare of your friends' choosing.

 11 Do an impression of someone in the room.

 12 Turn your clothes inside out and wear them like that for the rest of the game.

FRIENDS

If you choose more than three dares in a row, you have to do a penalty dare. Throw one of the dice to see which dare you have to face.

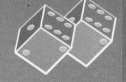

PENALTY DARES

These must be done as soon as possible (obviously not during school!).

1 Do a stupid walk in public.

2 Go out in your mom's clothes.

3 Do not say "yes" for the next hour.

4 Wear your top inside out for the whole day.

5 Outline your lips with lipstick and walk into a store.

6 Walk down the street backward, passing at least two people.

ARGUMENTS

Even the best of friends argue sometimes. It hurts. It stinks. But it happens. So here are some tips to get you talking again.

1. BE SPECIFIC AND STICK TO THE POINT

You need a discussion and then an agreement, not another shouting match. Approach your friend calmly and be tactful. Say your piece and listen to her point of view.

DO SAY "Your friendship means a lot to me and I don't want this to come between us."

DON'T SAY "I can't believe you did/think that. I hate you!"

2. KEEP CALM

Remember to breathe! However angry you are, speak slowly and make yourself understood.

DO keep eye contact.
DON'T stare at the floor and fidget.

3. APOLOGIZE IF YOU'RE THE ONE AT FAULT

Cut the Little Miss Innocent act. No one is perfect. If you've done something wrong, accept that your friend has every reason to be upset.

DO SAY "I realize I was wrong and I'm sorry." Then listen to what she has to say.

DON'T SAY "Look, I might have been wrong but you made it worse." (That is not an apology!)

Note: Avoid endless apologizing. Everyone messes up occasionally.

4. DON'T GIVE IN TOO EASILY

Some people back down and beg for forgiveness at the first sign of a fight, even when they have done nothing wrong.

DO be prepared to stand your ground if you are in the right.
DON'T apologize for being alive!

5. DON'T EXPECT THINGS TO BE STRAIGHTENED OUT RIGHT AWAY

Arguments are messy, and it can take time to work things through.

DO respect her wishes if your friend doesn't want to talk about the situation, but let her know it's upsetting you.
DON'T force her to talk things through. It will lead to another argument.

6. COMPROMISE

If you've argued because you want to do different things, find a middle ground you're both happy with.

DO stick to it. Your friendship is more important than getting your way all the time, isn't it?
DON'T moan and complain about it afterward!

7. REAL FRIENDS DON'T KEEP SCORE

If there is a competition going on, for grades, looks, or clothes, it's a pattern you need to stop.

DO SAY "Game over. Let's do things together, not compete."
DON'T SAY "I bet you won't stick to it." If competition is the only thing your friendship is based on, that's not good.

8. AGREE TO DISAGREE

You're individuals and you're not going to agree about everything. As soon as you realize that, you're going to get along a lot better.

DO SAY "I think differently and we're all allowed to be different."
DON'T SAY "You're crazy to think that."

GOOD VS. BAD

A test of friendship

Most friends have good and bad points. If your friend's bad ones start chipping away your confidence, it's time for a few changes. See if any of these descriptions match your friend.

BOSSY BOOTS

SHE'S THE ONE WHO . . . takes control of everything and always gives you advice, whether or not you ask for it. **YOU LOVE HER BECAUSE . . .** she's mega-honest, well-meaning, and full of ideas. **SHE ANNOYS YOU BECAUSE . . .** she's so bossy that you've started to think your own opinions are totally worthless. **TRY . . .** suggesting things to do, so she doesn't make all the decisions all of the time. And tell her when she's being too in-your-face. **DROP HER WHEN . . .** she won't listen to anything you say.

76

SNEAKY PAL

SHE'S THE ONE WHO . . . is as nice as pie to your face, but not so nice behind your back. **YOU LOVE HER BECAUSE** . . . she's fun and good to hang out with. **SHE ANNOYS YOU BECAUSE** . . . she can be mega-nasty. It seems as if she lacks confidence, because she puts you down to try and make herself feel good. **TRY** . . . laying down the law. Make it clear that you won't stand for being dissed behind your back. **DROP HER WHEN** . . . she starts making you miserable.

SULK MONSTER

SHE'S THE ONE WHO . . . acts fine when things go her way, but lets darkness descend the minute she doesn't agree with something. **YOU LOVE HER BECAUSE** . . . she's great when she's in a good mood. She's someone you can always turn to. **SHE ANNOYS YOU BECAUSE** . . . she can get very huffy. And let's face it, it doesn't take much to put her on a one-way train to Mood Central. **TRY** . . . letting her know her sulk sessions are getting you down. If she knows they affect you, she should try to put on a brave face. **DROP HER WHEN** . . . the gloomy moods outnumber the giggly ones. It's NO fun having to walk on eggshells all the time.

77

COPYCAT COPYCAT

SHE'S THE ONE WHO . . . simply can't bear to go anywhere without you. And she copies all your outfits. **YOU LOVE HER BECAUSE** . . . when the rest of your pals are busy, she'll always come over for gossip or a video. **SHE ANNOYS YOU BECAUSE** . . . your other friends think you're actually the same person. **TRY** . . . explaining that she's a very special friend but you need your own space, too. **DROP HER WHEN** . . . you feel like you've got a stalker.

PAL DROPPER

SHE'S THE ONE WHO . . . drops you when someone cooler (or so she thinks) come along. **YOU LOVE HER BECAUSE** . . . when you're in favor you feel fab. **SHE ANNOYS YOU BECAUSE** . . . she'll put your friendship completely on hold and start piling attention on the new girl at school. **TRY** . . . telling her you're not prepared to be her friendship flavor of the month. **DROP HER WHEN** . . . you realize she's not going to change. You're worth more than that, you know.

CUTTING LOOSE

When it's time to say good-bye

This is probably the hardest thing to do, but sometimes you realize that a friendship is not a good one, especially if it is causing you pain, worry, or upset. Be honest with yourself and your friend (that means talking to her, not complaining to everyone else about her). If it's really not in your best interests to hang on to a friend, then that's your cue to cut her loose. Take what you've learned from this friendship into your next one and make sure that whoever you choose to give your friendship to will return it 100%.

TEN EASY WAYS TO LOSE FRIENDS

1 Agree wholeheartedly when your friend says, "I acted like a total idiot."

2 Immediately drop your friend the minute someone cooler walks into the room.

3 Become a total bore. Constantly whine and complain about everything and everyone.

4 Act jealous whenever she spends time with other people.

5 Envy everything from how she looks to the grades she makes in school, so she no longer enjoys your company.

6 Demand that she tell you absolutely everything, then immediately tell everyone else.

7 Criticize her and try to change her.

8 Never be there when she needs you, but always expect her to be there for you.

9 Constantly make fun of her.

10 Turn into her clone.

FRIENDSHIP CHARMS

Just for fun!

Friendship charms are simple, innocent, and fun to do.

THE "BEST FRIENDS FOREVER" CHARM

This is a bonding charm for you and your friend. Make sure you won't be interrupted or it will weaken the bond.

ALL YOU NEED: 1 pink ribbon, 2 pens, 1 white plate, 2 pink marshmallows, and a pair of scissors

WHAT TO DO:

1 Both of you take turns writing on the pink ribbon. Write some words that sum up your friendship. These can be as strange or as silly as you like — they just need to mean something to both of you.

2 Place the ribbon on the white plate.

3 Now eat the marshmallows.

Chew each marshmallow ten times before you swallow it. Between eating each marshmallow, repeat the following words:

"May our friendship be as mellow and sweet as this food we love to eat."

4 Cut the ribbon in half and each of you keep one half somewhere safe. Every so often, you can get together to repeat this spell. Bringing along a friendship token will make it extra special.

THE LETTER CHARM

Use this when you just want to let her know what a fab friend she is.

ALL YOU NEED: Writing paper, pen, envelope, postage stamp, a rose or butterfly sticker or stick-on tattoo (if you can't find one of these, you can always draw it yourself).

WHAT TO DO:

1 Stick the butterfly or rose onto the piece of paper and write a few friendly words.

2 Seal it in the envelope, put on the stamp, and write your friend's address.

3 As you mail the letter, imagine hot, pink light whizzing off of your letter. Keep sending positive thoughts throughout the day. Before sunset the next day, you will find your friendship feels stronger than ever.

THE HEALING CHARM

Use this when you want to make up after an argument with your friend.

ALL YOU NEED: Green, pink, and orange ribbons (each long enough to go three and a half times around your wrist), and a thread from your friend's clothing or a hair from her head.*

* It may be hard to get a thread or a hair. Think smart — check out where she's been sitting or look at something she's borrowed from you. If not, you can do the spell *without* the thread or hair.

1 Once you've got the thread or hair, the rest is simple. Sit down by yourself in a quiet place. Pick up your three ribbons and begin to braid them together while saying:

"As these ribbons I twist and twine, so will my dear friend again be mine."

2 When you get halfway along the ribbon, begin to braid the thread or hair in with the rest (optional).

3 When you've finished braiding, tie a knot to keep the ends in place. As you do this, say your friend's name aloud three times.

4 Twist the band you've made three times around your left wrist and tie it. Wear it at all times and you'll be buddies again. If nothing has happened after a few days, try giving the bracelet to your friend as a peace offering and let the magic work on her directly (for a *real* way to patch things up, go to page 74).

BE PERFECT PALS

If you're tired of fighting with friends, or your pals seem to be constantly at each others' throats, here's how to make sure you remain perfect pals.

1. SHOW EACH OTHER YOU CARE

How does it feel when someone pays you a compliment? Nice, huh? Make sure your friends know how great they are, too.

2. BE YOURSELVES

Don't change your tastes to match each other. You are individuals, not clones. You love one another just as you are.

3. REMEMBER TO MEET HALFWAY

If you do argue with your friends, or they argue with each other, don't panic. It's perfectly normal and very healthy to have different views about things. You can always agree to disagree or at least try to meet in the middle (see page 74 for how to deal with disagreements).

4. SECRETS ARE SACRED

Always keep your friends' secrets. Trust is the basic ingredient of lasting friendships. You'll probably be sharing lots of new experiences with your best buds over the next few years, so make sure you keep their secrets safe. Forever.

5. HAVE FUN!

The golden rule of friendship is to have a good time together. If you can make your friends collapse on the floor in a heap of giggles just by looking at them, you know you've got something special.

PEARLS OF WISDOM

A GREAT FRIENDSHIP IS . . . one where you don't have to explain everything.

Listen to your friends even when you think you can't listen another minute. After all, you'll want your friends to listen to you when you're whining . . . er . . . droning on . . . er . . . sorry — you know what I mean!

Be a true friend and help to patch up any disagreements between your friends.

Don't turn away a PNF (potential new friend) just because she's not a soul mate. She could be great fun.

It's better to lose an argument than to lose a friend.

84

DESTINY

What does the
future hold?

YOUR DESTINY

How often do you daydream about what will happen in the future? Well, if you're like most people, the answer is a lot of the time. Thinking about what's in store is natural. Even the most cynical among us can't help peeking at our horoscopes to find a clue about what's going to happen.

In this chapter, you'll get tips on how to trust your gut feelings and open your mind to possibilities. Then it's up to you to make those possibilities a reality.

The most important thing to remember is that this chapter doesn't hold all the answers. Only *you* can truly determine what happens in your life. But let this chapter stir all your senses into exploring what you really want and what you're capable of achieving.

So now relax, clear your mind, and prepare to peek into your destiny. And remember, always go with your instincts and be true to yourself!

AN ASTROLOGICAL GUIDE

The next five years revealed

We all want to know what's around the next corner, whether it's an A in math, a new pair of jeans, an argument, or a new friend. But it's harder to think about what's going to be happening over the next five years. It's impossible to know for sure, but using what we know about ourselves and a little astrology, we can have fun guessing.

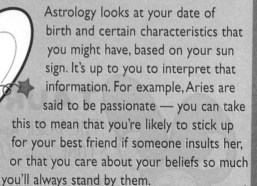

Astrology looks at your date of birth and certain characteristics that you might have, based on your sun sign. It's up to you to interpret that information. For example, Aries are said to be passionate — you can take this to mean that you're likely to stick up for your best friend if someone insults her, or that you care about your beliefs so much you'll always stand by them.

Turn the page to find your sign.

ARIES THE RAM March 21 to April 19
STONE Ruby   COLORS Bright reds

YOU

You're a strong individual with lots of
energy, and you're not afraid to take
risks. Over the next couple of years
you're likely to make lots of new friends.
You're also determined and logical, so although
you might find yourself with a hobby that is a
little out of the ordinary, you'll approach it in the
same way you approach your math homework.

FAMILY AND FRIENDS

You're a sentimental and emotional person who
has very close ties with family and one or two friends.
These relationships will only get better over time, but within a few years
you'll find that some of the people who are in your group right now
might not be your closest friends in the future. But that'll be your
choice — you don't always need people as much as they need you.

LOVE

Aries girls are very passionate, tactile, and loyal. You will fall head over
heels in love and enjoy amazingly happy times, but you'll also feel let
down occasionally.

TAURUS
THE BULL April 20 to May 20
STONE Jade   COLORS Green, cream

YOU

You're determined and devoted to whatever it is you
do, so although work might be a struggle sometimes,
in the next five years it'll come more easily and you'll
reach your goals. You like to fit in.

FAMILY AND FRIENDS

You love your group of friends and they know they can turn to you whenever they're in trouble. There's no reason to expect that your social group will change much over the next five years. But be careful; if you do have tension with a friend, you're likely to keep your anger bottled up — for ages! This could be a problem, because at some point you might explode and then your friend might not be able to forgive such an outburst. Taurus girls are often close to their families, but you are stubborn, and the only way to avoid Mom and Dad shouting is to force yourself to be more flexible.

LOVE

Taurus girls get along with all different kinds of people and will have lots of good friendships with boys. When you find your soul mate, you will be friends forever. When Taurus girls love, they love with all their heart.

GEMINI THE TWINS May 21 to June 21

STONE Tiger's eye

COLORS Black and white together, sharp yellow

YOU

Geminis are always ready for a laugh and don't take anything seriously. You're also really spontaneous and love having ten projects going at once. This is fine at first, but you're not Supergirl and you may struggle to juggle everything. Gemini girls change their minds regularly about what they want to do. Your saving grace is that you're so charming that you can get away with almost anything. People trust you and look up to you, so expect a leadership role in the future.

FAMILY AND FRIENDS

You're Miss Popular and everyone wants to be your friend. Your circle of friends will just get bigger and bigger, and in the next five years you'll be invited everywhere and will be partying nonstop.

LOVE

Gemini girls are destined to search for true love for a long time, but you'll have lots of fun along the way. When you do find your dream boy, you'll know not to let him go.

CANCER THE CRAB June 22 to July 22

STONE Moonstone COLORS Pastels, silver

YOU

You're a very sensitive person, which means you are generous, tolerant, and compassionate, but it also means you're afraid of being hurt. This can cause problems for a Cancer girl, because instead of getting out there and socializing, you're likely to hide away. By not taking risks, you might be stopping yourself from achieving your goals. Cancer girls are logical and safe. You'll do well in your exams because you're aware of what you're good at.

FAMILY AND FRIENDS

Cancer girls are very maternal and they take care of their friends and family. You make people very happy because they know they can always depend on you, although they may encourage you to be a bit more impulsive over the next couple of years.

LOVE

Because Cancer is the sensitive sign, you may have a rocky road to true love, but one day you'll be adored by someone who truly cares for you.

LEO THE LION

July 23 to August 22

STONE Citrine COLORS Orange, gold

YOU

Leo girls are natural leaders, so you're already making a big impact at school. You're probably doing well in your favorite subjects and are already certain of what you want later on. Be careful, though — Leos have a tendency to let people know what they're good at, which can be seen as arrogance. You're spontaneous, lively, and love excitement, so expect the unexpected over the next five years.

FAMILY AND FRIENDS

At home, you're proud of your bedroom, which is great for you but not so good for your little brother or sister if they dare to invade your space. This sometimes goes for your parents, too. Leos hate apologizing, so this can cause friction at home.

LOVE

Leo girls are usually very popular, so you'll have lots of boys interested in you. You can afford to be fussy, so don't settle for second best.

• •

VIRGO THE MAIDEN August 23 to September 22

STONE Agate COLORS Green, light brown

YOU

You're gentle, self-analytical, and shy. Virgo girls always do well in their schoolwork because they strive to do their best. You're happier taking a backseat and you're super-organized, so it's very likely that you'll end up supporting a highly successful person or enterprise in some way.

91

FAMILY AND FRIENDS

You're close to your family — you need them and you need their attention. If everything's happy at home over the next five years, you'll feel content and secure, but if not, or if any of your family is critical of you, you could have miserable moments. You can be oversensitive, not only with your family but with everyone. You're very choosy about your friends, and some people might see you as a bit of a snob. But you just know who you are and what you like. So expect a bumpy but exciting life in the next five years — your Virgo charm will get you through anything.

LOVE

Virgo girls are always looking for love and romance, but because you're picky, you won't always find it. Don't panic — you *will* find true love!

LIBRA THE SCALES September 23 to October 23
STONE Opal COLORS Pink, blue

YOU

You're friendly, caring, and attentive and really happy only when you're with other people. Also, as the sign of the scales, you're great at weighing options. In the next few years this will come in very handy. You'll make excellent choices at school and you'll be the one in the group who'll settle all the arguments. Libra girls don't like confrontation, which can be a good thing. You're likely to get along with people who'll help you succeed in the future.

FAMILY AND FRIENDS

You are very dependent on your friends, and if you don't get to see them regularly, you get upset. The next few years with them will be the basis for great long-term friendships. These girls will always remember your good advice and all the times you were there for them.

LOVE

Libra girls are attentive, gentle, and loving. You're wise, too — so you're more set on getting to know yourself first, before throwing yourself into love.

● ●

SCORPIO THE SCORPION October 24 to November 21
STONE Jasper COLORS Dark red, black

YOU

You've got a very strong personality. People know you're trustworthy and able to get what you want in life. You like to be a leader. You've probably got a game plan for the next five years, even if you don't know it! And you're doing everything you can to do well at school. Work is your passion, and your success shows people how determined you are. You don't like wasting time, so expect to have five busy years ahead, jam-packed with outside interests and extra schoolwork. Scorpio girls are also the first among their friends to get a part-time job and start earning money.

FAMILY AND FRIENDS

You're close to your family and have a large group of pals, but you're not clingy with them. You need space and, as long as they understand that, you should have very few arguments in the next few years.

LOVE

Scorpio girls are warm and affectionate. You'll meet lots of fun boys but won't be pinned down until you spot your true love.

SAGITTARIUS THE ARCHER

November 22 to December 21
STONE Amethyst COLORS Purple, autumnal colors

YOU

You're confident, creative, and optimistic. People like being around you because you're honest, tolerant, and enjoy doing new things. But you do tend to think that whatever you do is right, even if your best friends disagree. This is what will cause you the most arguments over the next five years. You're probably the one in class who gets involved in debates and is confident enough to put a hand up whether you know the answer or not!

FAMILY AND FRIENDS

You're sociable and the best listener of all the signs. Your friends love you and they let you know it. But you will have moments of frustration. Taking on friends' problems can leave you exhausted!

LOVE

Sagittarius girls need to find out about the world and themselves before they are prepared to share that with anyone else. When you're ready, love will come your way fairly easily.

CAPRICORN THE GOAT

December 22 to January 19
STONE Jet COLORS Black, gray

YOU

You know exactly what you want and you're determined to get it. You're hard-working and

you learn from your mistakes. Whether it's schoolwork, saving money, or playing sports, you always achieve your goals. You like to look good and you're very concerned about people's opinions of you.

FAMILY AND FRIENDS

Capricorn girls are faithful to their families and generally you all get along very well. You can get caught up in your own little world and aren't always aware of the effect your actions have on others. But in the next three years, you will become more thoughtful and will be very close to your family again. It's the same with your friends, but they are more forgiving because they know you're a true friend.

LOVE

When it comes to boys, Capricorn girls are overemotional. You can be shy with the boys you really like, but can't we all sometimes? When you do fall in love, you'll be able to show your feelings.

AQUARIUS THE WATER BEARER

January 20 to February 18
STONE Garnet COLORS Bright pink, electric green

YOU

You're original, independent, and full of ideas. At the moment, you may feel that school restricts your ideas and has too many rules for you. In five years, your individuality and eccentricity will be rewarded, but until then, you're going to have to argue your case. Sometimes you may lose, but don't let that deter you — people will admire your spirit!

95

FAMILY AND FRIENDS

You flit between enjoying your group and needing time alone. At home your parents think you're being moody when you disappear into your room, but they also realize that it's just the way you are. You can be a little tactless, so although your friends love being around you, you can upset them sometimes. You will be the first of your friends to find your own style.

LOVE

Aquarius girls like their freedom, so in a few years you won't understand why your friends put so much emphasis on boyfriends. But when the time is right, you will fall head over heels in love.

PISCES THE FISH February 19 to March 20
STONE Carnelian   COLORS Silver-blue, gray

YOU

You're considerate, dreamy, and romantic. You're never in a hurry and although people think you're vague, you do get things done. You're very giving, but you're creative, too. At school you're learning to manage your time and workload; in the next few years, this skill will be invaluable.

FAMILY AND FRIENDS

Your untidiness is going to be the key to most of your family fights. But your family adores you and you're at your happiest at home. Being so open with your friends will pay off — those friendships should stand the test of time.

LOVE

When a Pisces girl finds Mr. Right, there is no other sign that will have such a perfect romance. Think of all your favorite sappy movies and triple the sappiness — that will be you!

RAD LIB

Here's a fun horoscope reading for you and your best friend. Separately, you should write down your answers to the following.

1 **Your zodiac sign** Libra
2 **A messy room in your house** my room
3 **A planet** Moon
4 **A talent you have** violin
5 **Another word for strange** weird
6 **An emotion** happy
7 **A bad feeling** when I'm wrong
8 **A good feeling** when I'm right
9 **Current month** January
10 **Current year** 2015
11 **Day of the week** wednesday
12 **Name of a family member** Sachit
13 **Number between 11 and 20** 16
14 **Number between 4 and 10** 8
15 **Something you dislike.** waking Day

NOW GO TO THE NEXT PAGE

RAD LIB REVEALED

Replace the numbers in the paragraph below with your answers to see your crazy rad lib horoscope prediction.

1 for the month of **9** of **10**: Looks like you're going to have a **5** month with **3** bumping into your House of **6**. Avoid speaking to **12** about money on any **11** — it will only lead to an argument. You are seeking **8** over **7** in the coming weeks. Don't be discouraged by what appears to be an onslaught of **15** at the end of the month. Resolve to clean **2** before the new moon and your worries will fade. You may find yourself being more protective of your **4** skills — look for a way to get things you need without exploiting yourself. Your best days this month are **14** and **13**.

WHAT'S YOUR ELEMENT ?

First check out which element your sign falls under. Then read on to find out what your element says about you.

FIRE (Aries, Leo, and Sagittarius)

You are . . . enthusiastic, impulsive, and energetic. You're also caring and friendly, although you can be loud and scare less outgoing people. **You sail through situations** . . . in which you have to be the leader and get everyone's enthusiasm totally soaring. **You stumble when** . . . you're in one-on-one situations with people you don't know. You can feel under pressure. **Try** . . . staying calm when you get nervous. It's OK to get wound up sometimes, but learn to chill and you'll feel a lot better.

EARTH (Taurus, Virgo, and Capricorn)

You are . . . practical, careful, and calm. It takes a lot to get you frazzled. You're a down-to-earth gal who likes to be around honest, approachable people. **You sail through situations** . . . when someone needs your undivided attention. You're a great listener and love quiet one-on-ones, especially if you're giving a friend advice.

You stumble when . . . you're in crowds, such as parties or family gatherings. You can find large groups quite daunting.

Try . . . to tell yourself, "I can do it." You'll start to feel more optimistic.

WATER (Cancer, Scorpio, and Pisces)

You are . . . thoughtful and have no trouble talking to new people. You also look for the best in people and it disappoints you when other people see only the bad. **You sail through situations** . . . that involve overcoming problems and keeping people happy. You find anything that involves talking to people a total breeze! **You stumble when** . . . you're thrown into something that goes wrong. Because you're thoughtful and intelligent, you don't like others to be sloppy or careless. **Try** . . . being less demanding and relax more. No one expects you to be perfect.

AIR (Gemini, Libra, and Aquarius)

You are . . . romantic, emotional, and ruled by your heart. Sometimes you can be a little too sensitive and your emotions can keep you from thinking things through properly. **You sail through situations** . . . that involve helping others or lending a sympathetic ear. You're a great friend to have when the going gets tough. **You stumble when** . . . a close friend acts out of character. You can also get uncomfortable meeting new people. **Try** . . . flattering yourself. You don't need other people to make you feel good! Set yourself achievable goals.

THE ORACLE

A chart of luck and fortune—just for fun!

The Oracle is a simple chart that suggests possible outcomes to questions spinning around in your mind. It also helps you uncover things that are lying around in your subconscious.

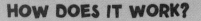

HOW DOES IT WORK?

Think carefully about questions you want answered. The Oracle will give you the answer. All you do is close your eyes, then toss a coin onto The Oracle at least five times. Keep a note of which squares your coin lands on. If it is mostly one square, there's your answer. If the coin lands equally between two squares, toss again. If the coin lands between three or four squares, the table is telling you that it's too early to discover the answer yet. Try again another day.

WHAT TO DO

You can ask up to six questions at any one time. Think hard, then write them down before you begin. You must ask The Oracle very specific things, e.g., Will we be friends again? Will I get better at English? Should I take singing lessons? Copy this table onto a large piece of paper or cardboard and fill in the squares as shown on the opposite page. Use a coin that fits comfortably into the squares to give an accurate reading. Now toss the coin and find out what The Oracle has to say. Then turn the page to see what it all means.

1

Yes, but put in more effort.

2

No, but in time.

3

If you believe in yourself.

4

Yes, but do you really want that?

5

Others are in the way now.

6

If you feel really positive.

7

You're not ready.

8

Yes, the time is right.

9

Yes, if you make a plan.

10

Your friends can help you.

11

Don't give up hope.

12

Follow your instincts.

WHAT THE ORACLE SAYS ABOUT YOU

The Oracle points toward what's really important to you. The order in which the questions popped into your head is a big clue.

THE FIRST QUESTION
This is what's most important to you right now.

THE SECOND QUESTION
This is what's bothering you the most.

THE THIRD QUESTION
The answer to this is the one that will be the most true.

THE FOURTH QUESTION
This is the deepest.

THE FIFTH QUESTION
This is the question that will affect your future the most.

THE SIXTH QUESTION
This is something that you think you want right now, but you may well change your mind in the near future.

LETTERS OF FORTUNE

It's all in your name

The letters of your name can reveal the person you could become. Here's how.

HOW IT WORKS

In the list that follows, there is a description next to each letter. The first letter in your name should be the most accurate description of you, but each letter is significant. As you go through all the letters in your name, you will build a picture of your personality and what your future may hold. If something is repeated, take notice!

WHAT TO DO

Get a pen and paper and write down the letters of your first name. Use the name you're most commonly called — for example, if Catherine is the name on your birth certificate but everyone calls you Cathy, use Cathy. Or if everyone calls you by a nickname, use that instead. Write down each description or prediction. If you think a description is inaccurate, ask a friend for a second opinion.

LETTERS OF FORTUNE

A Your enthusiasm is inspiring. You can travel far and achieve your dreams through hard work and skill.

b You're honest and outspoken, but you should think before you act.

C You are understanding and wise, so people look up to you. You tend to ignore small problems in the hope that they will go away.

d You're very good at settling arguments between others. You're also a risk taker, which could lead to riches if you are clever.

e You're calm and versatile, which makes people respect you. You shouldn't feel insecure about what others think of you.

f You're good at making friendships last — and some will last you a lifetime. You enjoy being part of a team.

g You like time alone but you connect with friends who share your interests. You're practical and cope well with any problems life may throw at you.

h You're talented and your friends admire you for that, but if you learn a little more humility, you will truly shine.

i You're warm and thoughtful toward others. You notice people's positives, and this will be important to your future.

j You've got the power to help others, so use it and you'll be happy. You have good intuition — rely on it.

k You're great to confide in and you always keep a secret. You're an independent soul.

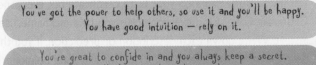

L You're seen as the spiritual one, so use your powers of intuition. Don't let envy prevent you from becoming close to people.

DESTINY

m
You need to feel comfortable and don't like new situations. Don't be tempted to play with other people's emotions — you'll regret it.

n
You worry about things that might never happen. The future holds good things for you, so stop worrying.

o
Keep being honest — friends appreciate it. Loyalty and love will keep you close to your friends, now and in the future.

p
You are down-to-earth and wise. Use that wisdom — don't waste it. Acting superior makes others feel insecure.

q
You always see people in the best light but sometimes expect too much. Be logical about situations that arise in the future.

R
You like to be creative and a bit wild. Your friends often go along with what you want, but don't persuade them to act selfishly.

S
You're great at getting things done, for others as well as yourself. Your greatest gift is that you make people happy.

t
You're lively and spontaneous. You always hope for closer relationships, but you don't stay still long enough.

u
You're a perfectionist, so you try to make everything, even friendships, just right. Don't be demanding, and they will be.

v
You're an individual and don't always go along with the crowd. You get bored easily, but if you make an effort for people, they will make an effort for you.

W
You're a great shoulder to cry on — one of the most dependable girls in your group. Never go along with foolish plans without thinking them through.

X
You love nothing more than being out with your friends. You can also be a bit of a dreamer. Stay grounded.

y
Take your friends' advice more often, otherwise you'll find yourself getting into trouble.

Z
You're observant and understand people well. You can be a little vain, so remember to be modest.

DESTINY

THE MARVELOUS MIND-READING GAME

Just how good are your mind-reading powers?

Dim the lights, focus your brain, and play on to find out.

YOU'LL NEED:
1. Between one and four pals   2. Psychic powers

HOW TO PLAY

This is a battle of the minds. Below are thirteen questions that you must answer — without anyone saying a word!

Decide who should start and then go through the questions one by one. You have to guess the answer your friend has in her mind. (And she must be honest!) If you get it right, move on to the next question. If you get it wrong, the person on your left gets to go. Each person has three tries at guessing a question. Write down who gets the right answers, and how many times they try, to see who has the best psychic powers.

MIND-READING TIPS

- Sit opposite the friend whose mind you are reading.
- Close your eyes.
- Put one hand on her head and try to see what she's thinking.
- Focus really hard — as hard as you possibly can.
- The answer should pop into your head. Good luck!

QUESTIONS

1 The friend on your left is thinking of a color. **Guess which one.**

2 The friend on your left is thinking of a female pop star. **Guess which one.**

3 The friend on your left is thinking of a sandwich filling. **Guess which one.**

4 The friend on your left is thinking of a sports star. **Guess which one.**

5 The friend on your left is thinking of a chocolate bar. **Guess which one.**

6 The friend on your left is thinking of a current pop music hit. **Guess which one.**

7 The friend on your left is thinking of a boy band. **Guess which one.**

8 The friend on your left is thinking of another one of your friends. **Guess which one.**

9 The friend on your left is thinking of a magazine. **Guess which one.**

10 The friend on your left is thinking of a soap opera. **Guess which one.**

11 The friend on your left is thinking of a movie star. **Guess which one.**

12 The friend on your left is thinking of a book. **Guess which one.**

13 The friend on your left is thinking of a boring subject. **Guess which one.**

ARE YOU PSYCHIC?

Can you see into the future or read people's minds? Read on to find out.

DO YOU EVER WAKE UP BEFORE THE ALARM GOES OFF IN THE MORNING?

a Never.
b Only if I'm really excited about something.
c Sometimes.
d Almost every day.

HAVE YOU EVER HAD A DREAM ABOUT SOMETHING THAT THEN REALLY HAPPENED?

a I wish.
b It has happened once.
c A few times.
d It happens regularly.

HAVE YOU EVER MET SOMEONE FOR THE FIRST TIME BUT FELT LIKE YOU KNEW THEM ALREADY?

a No — that sounds weird.
b Yes, but then I remembered I had met them before.
c I think so.
d Yes, it was a really strong feeling.

ARE YOU LUCKY?

a I once won a runner-up prize in a raffle.
b I once came in first in a competition.
c I've won quite a few competitions and raffles.
d I win everything I enter.

DO YOU KNOW WHAT YOUR BIRTHDAY PRESENT IS BEFORE YOU UNWRAP IT?

a Yes, but that's normally because I find where my mom has hidden it.

b Yes, but that's because I've asked for something specific.

c I usually guess it right.

d I know what it is just by looking at it.

EVER OPEN A DRAWER AND PULL OUT THE THING YOU'RE LOOKING FOR RIGHT AWAY?

a No way! It's normally in the last place I look.

b Very rarely.

c Sometimes.

d I don't ever need to look! I put my hand in and it's the first thing I touch.

DO YOU KNOW WHAT SOMEONE'S GOING TO SAY BEFORE THEY SAY IT?

a No! How would I know that?

b Only if it's a really good friend or family member.

c Sometimes, and it's really weird.

d I don't just know what they're going to say, I know what they're thinking, too.

WHAT DID YOU CHOOSE?

Mostly **a**s
It looks like you don't have many psychic abilities, or maybe you just haven't found them yet!

Mostly **b**s
You've got a little bit of intuition, but you're going to have to work at developing any psychic power.

Mostly **c**s
You're a little bit psychic, but is it all just luck and coincidence? Well, that depends on what you believe!

Mostly **d**s
You definitely have psychic powers; make sure you use them wisely!

ISLAND DREAMS

Take a trip into your mind

Picture yourself all alone on a beautiful desert island. You are happy and smiling. You can feel the warm, sandy beach under your feet, hear the waves lapping at the shore, and see the palm trees swaying gently in the cool island breeze. The sun is setting and the sky is filling up with a million bright stars.

Keep that image in your mind's eye as you answer the questions below on a separate sheet of paper.

How many palm trees can you see on the island?

Which of the following things on the island do you feel most drawn to?

| Sky | Palm trees | Sun | Stars | Sea |

Which two friends or family members do you wish were with you on your fantasy desert island?

Which three songs would be permanently playing on your Desert Island Discman?

TURN THIS PAGE UPSIDE DOWN TO SEE WHAT THE FUTURE HAS IN STORE FOR YOU

ISLAND FRIENDS

The first person you thought of is the one you feel closest to. The second is the person you would like to spend more time with.

SONGS

THE FIRST SONG tells you what the future holds for you. **THE SECOND SONG'S** title or a line in the song should answer a question that has been bugging you lately. **THE THIRD SONG** is all about what is on your mind at the moment.

PALM TREES

The number of palm trees you see is the number of days until you meet someone who's going to make a big impression on you.

WHAT YOU WERE MOST DRAWN TO

This represents your outlook on life.

SKY — Open-minded
PALM TREES — Career-minded
SUN — Kindhearted
STARS — Ambitious
SEA — Happy-go-lucky

DESTINY

FENG SHUI

*Improve your bedroom—
Improve your life*

Feng Shui is the Eastern art of balancing and improving the flow of natural energies in our surroundings to make life happier. If you rearrange some things, it could have a positive impact on your friendships or your mind. So bring a little Feng Shui into your life.

ENERGIZE YOUR ROOM!

You go to sleep there at night and it's the first place you see when you wake up. It's your haven when everyone's driving you crazy and it's the place where you spend most of your time. It's not surprising, then, that your bedroom can have a huge effect on you.

So if you think you need a little more energy to perk you up, then shut your door and get ready to do some rearranging.

YOUR BED

NOW: Your bed sits randomly in the middle of the room, just where your dad unpacked it five years ago, and the headboard is covered in old Barbie stickers that you haven't bothered to take off yet.

TRY: The position of your bed can seriously affect the vibe of your room. According to experts, it shouldn't be directly opposite the door, and it shouldn't face any mirrors. So put it on the same wall as the door, or diagonally across, for a more chilled-out feel. And get rid of those stickers!

YOUR FURNITURE

NOW: Your chest of drawers, desk, and everything else are all stuck in a row across from your bed to create maximum dance space in the middle of the room (under those piles of clothes that are probably on your floor!).

TRY: The mirror on your dresser can affect the energy levels in your room. It shouldn't face the bed or the door directly, because this stops good energy from flowing around the room. Put your dresser in a corner and, if there's room, put your chest of drawers on the same wall as your bed — any big corners pointing at the bed means bad vibes!

YOUR DOOR

NOW: Its paint is peeling and it's covered in old stickers, posters, and scribbles from the last hundred years or so. Everybody winces when you open it because it squeaks so much. Apart from that, it's looking pretty good!

TRY: Your door is the gateway into your room, so spend some extra time on it. First, try to persuade your folks to let you give it a fresh coat of paint — a color that matches the rest of your room. Then decorate it with a FEW things you like — a poster or two, a name plaque, or even a stencil if you're feeling artsy!

YOUR STUFF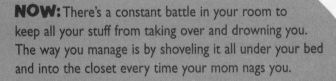

NOW: There's a constant battle in your room to keep all your stuff from taking over and drowning you. The way you manage is by shoveling it all under your bed and into the closet every time your mom nags you.

TRY: You need space in your room for the new "chilled-out" you. So get organized. Give everything a place in your closet or on a shelf and *put it back there!* Be ruthless with your old clothes. Do you really need that sparkly top that hardly fits and which you haven't worn for ages? Simply chuck it and enjoy the extra space (but check with your mom first).

YOUR FAVORITE THINGS

NOW: You've got tons of posters and pictures up, but the posters are turning yellow at the edges. Plus the pop stars you've put up are so out of date, it's getting embarrassing!

TRY: Take everything off the walls and start again. Make yourself some new artwork to show off your skills, and pull some swanky posters out of your favorite magazines to brighten the place up. Only put things you really like on display — after all, it's your room and it should show off exactly what kind of girl you are.

PLANTS AND GREENS

NOW: If you've made all those changes, your room should be a calm, relaxing place. But you do need a little extra energy in there as well to help you start the day. Plants are a great source of energy, but at the moment you've got only a half-dead fern that you water once a year . . . if it's lucky.

TRY: Go with your mom to the supermarket and get some cool-looking potted plants — ones with rounded leaves are the best for bedrooms because they don't give off *too* much energy. Put them around your room and enjoy those good vibes!

GENERAL FENG SHUI TIPS
- **Don't have anything on display that reminds you of bad times.**
- **Keep your room as clutter-free as possible.**

115

YOUR BEDROOM SECRETS

Did you know your bedroom reveals a lot about you? Read on to find out what.

DESTINY

PLANT

If your plant's healthy, you're the caring type. You always make sure your friends and family are OK. If it's a little wilted, you've probably got a lot on your mind and are distracted.

CD PLAYER OR RADIO

If your CD player is on display, you always notice what's going on around you. If it's hidden away, you tend to be a little less attuned to your surroundings.

UNDER YOUR BED

If there is a pile of junk under your bed, you may put off dealing with things in your life. The cleaner the space, the more likely you are to deal with your problems head-on.

DIARY

Keeping a journal shows that you take your emotions seriously. If you leave it out where anybody (especially a curious sis) could find it, you're literally an open book.

JEWELRY

An overflowing jewelry box means that you like taking care of your appearance. If you don't have much jewelry, you probably don't enjoy the limelight.

BED

If you make your bed every day, it means you're a no-nonsense kind of girl. If not, you may have some problems you're doing your best to ignore.

DESK

If you have a computer or a calculator prominently displayed, it means you're willing to embrace all things new. If you just have books, folders, and pens on your desk, it shows you're good with your hands.

POSTERS

An action picture, like one of a snowboarder, means you love speed, power, and expensive things. If you have a poster by a famous painter, you're a dreamer, whereas if you've pinned up a shot of your favorite band, you've got music on your mind.

CLOSET

If your closet is very neat with everything carefully hung up or nicely folded away, you can be very strict with yourself and others. If it's extremely messy, it means you're a bit of a rebel. And if it's somewhere in between, then you're laid-back.

PHOTOS

You can tell how you really feel about the people whose photos you have on display by looking at the frames holding them. The thicker the frame, the closer the friendship. Sticking a photo on a mirror means you see that person as a reflection of yourself. And if you've got your photos in a collage or on a bulletin board, you're very close to your friends and think of them as a team.

YOUR DREAMS REVEALED

Are your dreams telling you something?

Have you ever had a dream that lingered long after you woke up or one that seemed so vivid but then faded as soon as you opened your eyes? Your dreams are your brain going into overtime, making sense of things that have happened to you during the day. They reveal your subconscious mind, and here's what your mind might be saying.

ACCIDENT

Oops! You've done something you shouldn't have. This dream can also indicate that you don't feel in control of your life.

ANIMALS

Running from wild animals means you're denying your true feelings. Dreams of birds mean your imagination is ready to take off!

BIRTH

You may be about to discover something, such as the solution to a problem.

CAGE

Something in your life, like a friendship or a crush, is making you feel trapped.

COLORS

Dark, drab colors mean you may be feeling a little down. Bright colors mean you're feeling on top of the world!

DEATH

Don't worry, it doesn't mean someone's going to die! It means something is coming to an end.

EATING

You finally understand why a big change has happened or is still happening in your life, and what's more, you're totally cool with it.

FAME AND FORTUNE

If you dream of being a star, or you're on stage and everyone is applauding, it might mean that your self-esteem needs a boost. Turn to page 28 now!

FEELINGS

Emotions in dreams are often feelings you're trying to ignore in waking life. If you dream you're angry with someone, then you probably are, even if you're not fully aware of it awake.

GARDENS

If everything in the garden is beautiful and peaceful, then the same goes for your condition right now. If the garden's messy, your life's due to take a turn for the better.

MONEY

Dreaming of bills means you may be about to come into some cash. Dreaming of coins means that money is holding you back from doing something.

WHY DON'T YOU . . . record your dreams?

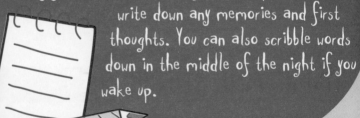

If you enjoy dream analysis, keep a pad of paper by your bed. As soon as you wake up, write down any memories and first thoughts. You can also scribble words down in the middle of the night if you wake up.

THE THREE MOST COMMON DREAMS EXPLAINED

YOU'RE FLYING

If you love flying in your dream, you're feeling confident. Otherwise, something is stopping you from getting where you want to be. Floating means you're feeling indecisive.

YOU'RE FALLING

You may be confused or worried. Falling fast and feeling scared may mean you're feeling insecure. Falling dreams are also a sign that you need to start enjoying yourself a little more.

YOUR TEETH FALL OUT

This dream marks the start of a new, responsible phase of your life. You're beginning to grow up and leave childish things behind you. If, in your dream, you feel anxious or even frightened, it means you're scared by the thought of getting older.

SUPERSTITIONS

We all know that walking under a ladder means bad luck, but did you know these superstitions? (Just for fun!)

FOR LUCK

If you spill salt, immediately scoop some up and throw it over your left shoulder.

When you climb into a car you should enter it with your right leg first for good luck.

A black cat crossing your path is unlucky. But if you just see a black cat, that's lucky.

Knock on wood for luck.

Seeing three butterflies together means good luck.

If you see a single magpie, that's unlucky. Tap your head and repeat, "Hello, Mr. Magpie, how are your wife and family?" three times for luck.

If, after leaving your house, you turn back to get something, you should sit down when you get indoors and count backward from seven to avoid bad luck.

Never put an umbrella on the bed.

FOR HEALTH

If you catch a falling leaf on the first day of autumn, you won't catch a cold that winter.

Have your hair cut on Friday to prevent headaches.

If you change your bed linens on a friday, you'll have strange dreams.

Never put new shoes on a table.

If you accidentally wear an item of clothing back to front or inside out, you are in for a great surprise.

Say "rabbits" three times before bed on the last day of a month and then say "hares" three times the next morning, and somebody will give you a present.

Pictures of an elephant bring luck, but only if they face the door.

If you use the same pencil for a school test that you used when you studied for it, you will do well on the test.

GOOD WISHES

If an eyelash falls out, put it on the back of your hand, make a wish, and throw it over your shoulder. If it flies off your hand, the wish will be granted.

If your right ear itches, someone is saying good things about you.

All wishes on falling stars come true.

If you see a cat with one eye, make a wish, spit on your thumb, and then stamp it in the palm of your hand. Your wish will then come true.

UH-OH!

If your left ear itches, someone is saying bad things about you.

If you spill pepper, you will have an argument with your best friend.

Never get out of bed on the side opposite to the one you got in or you will have a bad day.

If you bite your tongue, it means you have recently told a lie.

RED-LETTER DAYS

SNEEZE ON A MONDAY,
you sneeze for danger
SNEEZE ON A TUESDAY, smile at a stranger
SNEEZE ON A WEDNESDAY, sneeze for a letter
SNEEZE ON A THURSDAY, something better
SNEEZE ON A FRIDAY, sneeze for sorrow
SNEEZE ON A SATURDAY, see your sweetheart tomorrow
SNEEZE ON A SUNDAY, and joy will follow.

MONDAY'S CHILD
is fair of face
TUESDAY'S CHILD is full of grace
WEDNESDAY'S CHILD is full of woe
THURSDAY'S CHILD has far to go
FRIDAY'S CHILD is loving and giving
SATURDAY'S CHILD works hard for a living
AND THE CHILD BORN ON SUNDAY is fair and
wise, good and gay.

LOVE AND MARRIAGE

If you see a robin flying overhead on Valentine's Day, you will marry a sailor. If you see a sparrow, you will marry a poor man and be very happy. If you see a goldfinch, you will marry a millionaire.

MARRIED IN WHITE, you have chosen right
MARRIED IN GRAY, you will go far away
MARRIED IN BLACK, you will wish yourself back
MARRIED IN RED, you will be full of dread
MARRIED IN GREEN, ashamed to be seen
MARRIED IN BLUE, you will always be true
MARRIED IN YELLOW, ashamed of your fellow
MARRIED IN BROWN, you will live in the town
MARRIED IN PINK, your spirit will sink.

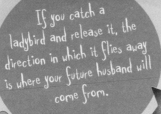

If you catch a ladybird and release it, the direction in which it flies away is where your future husband will come from.

If you count how many seeds are inside an apple, that is the number of children you will have.

If you want to find out who your future husband will be, stand on the sidewalk, wait until you've seen ten red cars, then a red-haired girl in a purple dress, then a man in a green tie. THEN the next young man you see will be your future husband.

Dropping a fork means a boy will come to visit.

Salty soup is the sign that the cook is in love.

MONEY

If a small spider crawls onto your clothes, you will come into some money.

It's bad luck to pick up a coin if it's tails side up. Good luck comes if it's heads up.

Never give someone an empty purse as a present. If you do, it will be empty forever.

If the palm of your right hand itches, it means you will soon be getting money. If your left palm itches, it means you'll lose money.

PEARLS OF WISDOM

Try not to go to sleep at night without settling an argument with your family or friends. Otherwise you'll only wake up in a bad mood.

Listen to what people you trust say about you. Your future will be rosier if you understand your weaknesses as well as your strengths.

YOUR future is in your hands!

DON'T SPEND YOUR TIME WORRYING ABOUT THE FUTURE. HAVE FUN TODAY!

OOPS!

Your cringe-free life
starts here!

OOPS!

OOPS!

ARE YOU A CRINGE QUEEN?

How mortifying!

Accidentally flashing your underpants to the world . . . It's happened to all of us at one time or another. But you can breathe a sigh of relief because *Pink Pages* is here to help you wave good-bye to your blushes.

Do you attract more than your fair share of shame?

START

You often put your foot in your mouth.

Yes → Remember the last time you fell down?

No → Remember the last time you fell down?

Yes ↓ Mom always asks you to do the dusting.

Your friends play tricks on you.

Yes ↓ You're told that your head is in the clouds.

No → Your parents embarrass you.

No ↑ Mom always asks you to do the dusting.

Yes ↓ Being organized is important to you.

130

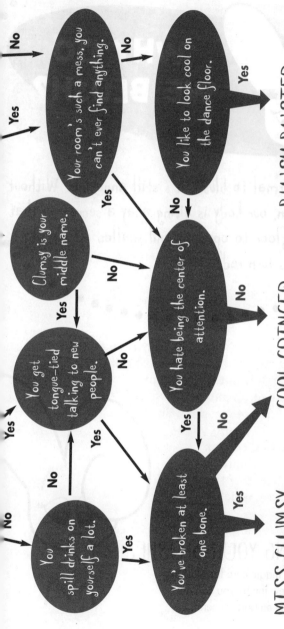

No → **Yes** → **No** → **Yes** → **No** → **Yes** → **No** →

You spill drinks on yourself a lot. — No / Yes

You get tongue-tied talking to new people. — Yes / No

Clumsy is your middle name. — Yes / No

You've broken at least one bone. — Yes

You hate being the center of attention. — Yes / No

Your room's such a mess, you can't ever find anything. — Yes / No

You like to look cool on the dance floor. — No / Yes

MISS CLUMSY
Whether you're tripping, slipping, or just saying the wrong thing, you go through life with a bright red face. But you've got a stack of funny stories to keep all your friends in stitches.

COOL CRINGER
You try your best to look cool and collected. But like most of us, you're not 100% safe from the Cringe Fairy. She strikes just when you least expect it.

BLUSH BUSTER
Wow! Do you own an anti-cringe spray? You never seem to suffer embarrassing moments or mishaps. Maybe you just don't get embarrassed easily. Lucky girl!

131

OOPS!

WHY DO WE BLUSH?

While it's normal to blush, it's still annoying. Without our permission, our body is giving away a secret — that we want the floor to open up and swallow us! So why do our cheeks turn red?

It's all about biology. When our body is faced with something that might be embarrassing, it doesn't know whether to tough it out or run. Your mind may want to up and leave, but your legs have other ideas. So to try to get you moving, your mind rushes blood to your muscles to make them faster and stronger. Some of this blood goes to your face, which explains the redness.

BANISHING YOUR BLUSHES

Sadly, there's no magic cure for blushing, but there are a few things you can do to try to lessen the embarrassment . . .

1 DON'T THINK ABOUT IT

Next time you feel your cheeks getting hot and red, start to think about something else. Try to remember a date from history class, or work out an equation. Before you know it, your blushes will have totally faded.

2 CREATE A DISTRACTION

Talk about something else. If everyone else sees you acting as if you're not bothered, they won't care, either.

3 LAUGH AT YOURSELF

Saving face is easy. Just shrug your shoulders and laugh as if you love nothing better than making a fool of yourself.

4 STAY CALM

Breathe properly and don't stress about the situation. It's really not as bad as you think. Even if it feels as if the whole world is laughing at you, they'll have forgotten about it tomorrow.

5 IT HAPPENS TO EVERYBODY

Remember, embarrassing stuff happens to everyone, including celebs (as you will see on pages 144–145). So hold your head high — you're in a cool club!

And if all the above fail and you just can't hide your flushed cheeks, then these work every time.

Wear a lot of red to provide the perfect camouflage.

OR Tell your friends you're experimenting with a new blush.

OR Tell them you've just finished jogging.

OOPS!

HOW WOULD YOU DEAL WITH IT?

Take this test to find out!

1. YOUR MOM BRINGS OUT AN EMBARRASSING BABY PHOTO OF YOU WITH NO CLOTHES ON TO SHOW TO YOUR FRIENDS. WHAT DO YOU SAY?

a "Mom! How *could* you?" Then stamp your foot and plunk yourself down on the couch with your arms crossed.

b "Oh, wasn't I just sooo cute!"

c "That's not me. That's my sister. Don't you know your own children, Mom?"

2. YOUR DAD INSISTS ON PERFORMING A POP SONG IN FRONT OF YOUR FRIENDS BUT GETS IT HOPELESSLY WRONG.

HOW DO YOU REACT?

a You stand rigid in the doorway, cringing with embarrassment, unable to move or speak.

b You shriek, "Isn't my dad just great? Don't you just want to hug him?" Then give him a big hug.

c You say, "Don't worry, Dad. Practice makes perfect. Come on, let's go watch MTV."

3. YOU'VE STARTED AT A NEW SCHOOL AND SOME GIRLS COME OVER TO TALK TO YOU. WHAT DO YOU DO?

a You can't speak. Your jaw sags slightly and you gaze at them openmouthed.

OOPS!

b You exclaim, "Wow! Do you want to hang out at lunch, then you could come to my house later and we could all walk to school together tomorrow?"

c You say "Hi" and are friendly.

4. YOUR FRIENDS ARE AT THE DOOR, BUT MOM INSISTS YOU WEAR AN UGLY BROWN RAINCOAT BEFORE SHE LETS YOU OUT. WHAT DO YOU DO?

a Shout at your mom, "It's hideous. I hate you!" before stomping off to your room, leaving everyone not knowing what to say or do next.

b Make a big deal of putting the raincoat on and parading around, striking poses like J-Lo.

c You say, "Thanks, Mom, but I'll be fine. I'm already wearing my parka, which has a hood, and I've got my umbrella if it really pours."

5. YOU'RE CHILLING OUT IN A FRIEND'S BEDROOM. YOU BEND DOWN TO PUT ON A CD WHEN, TO YOUR COMPLETE SURPRISE, YOU FART LOUDLY. (THERE'S NO POLITE WAY OF PUTTING THIS. SORRY!) IT'S THE MOST EMBARRASSING THING YOU'VE EVER DONE. HOW DO YOU REACT?

a You run out of the room, out of the house, all the way back to your own room, where you intend to hide for the rest of your life.

b One by one, all your friends start laughing. You join in the laughter until you are rolling around the floor, shrieking hysterically, tears pouring from your eyes.

c You say calmly, "Oops! Sorry." You then put on your fave music and act like nothing happened.

OOPS!

do you deal or squeal? turn the page to find out . . .

ANSWERS

Mostly **a**s

You NEED this chapter like peanut butter needs jelly. But there is hope for you. Try to RELAX. Remember that running away is not cool and it certainly doesn't solve anything. No one has ever (to my knowledge, anyway) died of embarrassment. And maybe things aren't quite as embarrassing or awful as you think they are.

Mostly **b**s

You usually bluff your way out of embarrassing situations by laughing it off. Humor is a great way out of any situation, but just make sure you don't use it to embarrass others and don't go overboard with the jokes.

Mostly **c**s

Awesome! You really know how to deal with the most terrible situations. You may not need this chapter, but why not read it, anyway? You might even pick up some new tips to add to your repertoire.

Every girl's surefire tips to

GET OUT OF EMBARRASSING SITUATIONS

1. **Keep smiling** So you got a zipper stuck trying on some jeans in the dressing room and the attendant had to rub soap on it just to get you out of them? Laugh about it,

and the world will laugh with you. If you see life as fun, people will want to hang out with you.

2. Be a trendsetter

You've dashed to your friend's house, and her dad answers the door. He says, "Nice outfit!" Then you realize you're still wearing your bunny slippers. Simply grin back and say, "Yeah, they're cool, aren't they?" Act confident even when you mess up, and others will follow your lead.

3. Act like a goof

Popular people are never scared to do silly things. So next time you walk into the classroom to find everyone giggling because you've got your skirt tucked in your underpants, just wink and wiggle your hips. It shows you know how to have fun and don't take yourself too seriously.

4. Love yourself

Sometimes it's hard to shrug off those feelings of shame. But next time you realize you've had a conversation with your crush with some broccoli stuck in your braces, don't spend the next month hiding in the corner. Keep a happiness diary instead. Every time you get a compliment or do something well, write it down. Then you can flip back through the pages any time to remind yourself how utterly wonderful you are.

5. Think about it in the right way

Wrong way of thinking about an embarrassing incident:

> *"I feel so STUPID! I hate myself. Everyone must think I'm so dumb, etc., etc. . . ."*

Right way of thinking about an embarrassing incident:

> *"Oh, well, it wasn't such a big deal. Everyone's probably forgotten about it already. It really doesn't matter."*

Armed with this attitude, you won't waste time sweating the small stuff.

OOPS!

137

LEARN FROM OTHERS' MISTAKES

Want to know what to do in the most embarrassing situations? Read and learn.

EMBARRASSING MOMENT

"The posters advertising my school's Halloween dance last year said there would be a prize for the best costume. My friend and I thought it was a good idea, so I went as a witch and she went as a vampire. When we walked into the main hall, everyone turned and stared. Even the DJ stopped the music. No one else was dressed up! We just ran straight back outside. Later we realized we'd read the wrong poster — the competition was for the younger kids, whose dance was the same afternoon! My class hasn't let me forget it."

HOW TO DEAL WITH IT

There's nothing worse than making a mistake in front of people at school, knowing you have to face them every day afterward. If you can't persuade your parents to move to a different country, then you're going to have to grin and bear it. Take a deep breath and go back. After all, now you've got a funny story to tell. Try to get people to laugh WITH you rather than at you. That way you'll influence their reactions and instantly feel better.

OOPS!

EMBARRASSING MOMENT

A couple of months ago, my mom and I went to the library and I got out a couple of joke books. Then we went to the supermarket and I told Mom some jokes as we walked around. Suddenly, I realized that my mom had walked off and I was telling jokes to a complete stranger! To make things worse, the other people near me were looking at me as if I were crazy!

EMBARRASSING MOMENT

When my mom and I were taking my little sister to preschool, my mom started talking to another mom. She was so busy talking that she didn't look where she was going. She slipped on some ice, landed flat on her butt, and pulled the other mom down with her. It took three people to help them up and my crush saw the whole thing. How embarrassing!

HOW TO DEAL WITH IT

When you have red-faced moments in public, remind yourself that the people around you are total strangers and you're not likely to see them again. Make yourself look at the people who are staring at you, smile, and walk off with your head held high.

HOW TO DEAL WITH IT

Your poor mom! Did you ask if she was hurt, or were you too busy hiding your head in shame? Sure, it must have been embarrassing to have your crush laugh at your mom, but I'm willing to bet it was a hundred times more embarrassing for her. Imagine how you would have felt if it were you. It's easy to laugh or feel ashamed when someone else is in an embarrassing situation, but try putting yourself in their shoes next time (and choose ones that don't slip!).

EMBARRASSING MOMENT

The other week my friend had a sleepover. I was nervous because I sleepwalk sometimes, but I tried not to think about it. Everything was fine until I woke up in the middle of the night, trying to get into her mom and dad's bed. I'd sleepwalked into their room! I don't know who was more embarrassed, me or them!

EMBARRASSING MOMENT

I wore a skirt to school one day and it kept creeping up, and I had to pull it down all day. As I was walking home I heard laughter behind me and thought my skirt had crept up again, but when I went to haul it down, it wasn't there! Then I realized it had gone right up to my waist and my underwear was on display!

HOW TO DEAL WITH IT

I'm surprised you could show your face in the morning! You must have wanted to hibernate and I bet your friends haven't let you hear the end of it. But I'm sure they realize you had no control over what you were doing — and if they don't, you must explain that. They may tease you for a while, but if they're real friends, they'll soon let it go. If they don't, let them know it's upsetting you. Don't suffer in silence.

HOW TO DEAL WITH IT

There's nothing more embarrassing than looking silly in public. If you still feel flustered every time you think about it, you'll find it much easier to cope if you tell people. Turning it into a funny story is much better than stressing about it. Just start off with, "You'll never guess what happened to me . . ." and take it from there.*

My mom and dad had friends over for dinner. After everyone had finished, I decided to make myself useful and clear the table. I got up from my chair, meaning to say, "Can I take your plates, please?" Instead I ended up saying, "Can I take your pants, please?" I had the reddest face ever!

I was walking up some stairs on the way to class when my hair suddenly caught on a boy's bag. I tried to pull it, but it was stuck. To make matters worse, he didn't notice and almost pulled me into his classroom. Even when I finally managed to yank it out, he had a chunk of hair stuck to his bag!

I was hanging around with some of my friends during lunch. We were standing and talking when I felt something warm on my head. You've guessed it — a bird had pooped all over my hair. I had to run to the bathroom and try to wash it off with tap water and paper towels. Everyone was staring at me, and the smell was terrible for the rest of the day.

OOPS!

TEN THINGS THAT MAKE YOU CRINGE

1
Walking around with toilet paper stuck to your shoe.

2

Your mom licking a hanky and wiping your face with it. In public.

3

Gossiping about someone in your class . . . and realizing she's standing right behind you.

4
All the boys in your class walking past while you're buying underwear.

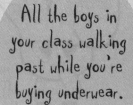

5

Your parents picking you up early from a party, especially when they come in and get you.

6

Calling your teacher "Mom" by accident. You just can't talk your way out of it!

7

Looking in the mirror at lunchtime only to find you've got toothpaste on your chin.

8

Your grandma saying, "I bet all the boys love you!" in front of everyone whenever she sees you.

9

Your mom making you try on really babyish clothes when you go shopping together.

10

Your parents getting out baby photos of you naked or dribbling in the bath whenever you have a sleepover.

OOPS! I'M A CELEBRITY
GET ME OUT OF HERE!

Let's face it: Most of us have made total idiots of ourselves in front of other people. Even seemingly perfe[c]t celebrities and superstars have had their fair share of goof-ups.

Katie Holmes had to act out an emotional scene where she had to try really hard to cry. Unfortunately, she got so into the scene that her nose started running. Take two!

Britney Spears was competing in a track meet at school. She was all pumped up and ready to go but was concentrating so hard she didn't hear the starting gun. As everyone else raced off, she was left standing there. Oops!

Avril Lavigne once got stuck in an airplane toilet. To add to her embarrassment, a film crew making a documentary about her had filmed the whole thing. Cut!

Spice Girl **Geri Halliwell** used to be a dancer in a club. One night she was up on a podium doing her thing when her leather pants ripped, revealing her underpants to the whole world. Not a good look!

OOPS!

144

Reese Witherspoon

will never live down her style disaster at her junior prom. Her old school friends happily tease her about her goofy smile, white shoes, tan tights, and awful blue dress. Pass the photos.

Sarah Michelle Gellar

went on a dinner date a while ago. She had been doing TV interviews all day and was so tired she yawned all the way through the appetizer. "By the time the meal arrived, I had my head on the table and was snoring my head off." Dating disaster!

Melissa Joan Hart lost her

super-cool image on the set of *Sabrina*. It was raining and she was trying to look smooth, but when she ran over to the side of the set, she slipped. Her feet came flying up and she landed on her butt. Ouch!

Renée Zellweger

was nowhere to be seen on live TV when Hugh Grant presented her with a Golden Globe Award. She had just slipped out to the bathroom. I'd just like to thank . . .

Orlando Bloom

remembers his first kiss as his most embarrassing moment. He was so unsure of what he was doing that they ended up bumping teeth. Kiss, kiss, clash!

Kate Winslet cringes when she remembers filming some scenes from *Titanic* with Leonardo DiCaprio. They had to spend hours in huge tanks of water and since it was too difficult to get out to use the bathroom, the unfortunate celebs had to relieve themselves in their clothes — in front of each other. Gross!

OOPS!

PEARLS OF WISDOM

Everyone has doubts and insecurities, even if they don't show them.

As you get more used to the embarrassing situations life is determined to throw at you, you will become more successful in keeping your cool.

No matter how embarrassing a situation is, no doubt someone, somewhere, shares your shame!

THE FIRST RULE OF COOL
It's not what you do, it's the way you do it.

THE SECOND RULE OF COOL
Regain your composure quickly and calmly.

THE THIRD RULE OF COOL
Don't try too hard to impress. You could end up being more fool than cool.

HELP

Got a dilemma?

GOT A PROBLEM?

Pink Pages is here to help!

Help! I want to be a rock star!

Better get busy.

- Start writing lyrics and melodies.
- Take every opportunity you can to perform.
- Take singing and music lessons. Teachers advertise in the local paper and music shops.
- Join a choir or a musical theater group. They will give you good voice training.

La La La La

Help! I never have any money to spend on friends' presents. How can I make it look like I've made more of an effort than I have?

Time to get artsy.
• Wrap up the present in pages from a magazine.
• Grab a small piece of plain paper and write a poem on it in your best handwriting.
   • Stick the poem on the present and — hooray! — a thoughtful gift.

Help! I want to change my room but I don't have a lot of money to spend.

Here are some ideas.

Photos look great displayed collage-style in a big frame or on a bulletin board.

• Hide clutter in storage boxes. Any boxes look good covered in wrapping paper, wallpaper, or fabric.

   • Drape a set of string lights around your mirror, headboard, or window. They'll give your bedroom a pretty glow at night.

      • A new carpet is expensive, so go for a big rug instead. It'll update your room in an instant.

         • Paint one wall a bright, vibrant color. Simple, cheap, but oh so effective.

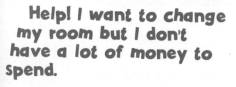

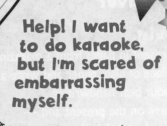

Help! I want to do karaoke, but I'm scared of embarrassing myself.

Follow these simple tips and you can't go wrong.

- For your voice to sound its best, hold the microphone a little away from your mouth. Imagine it's an ice-cream cone.
- If you're unsure of the words, don't dance, just concentrate on your singing. Or if you really feel the need to move, gesture with your hands and keep your feet still.
- Stick to what you know when picking tracks — at least that way you've got some chance of actually sounding like the song you mean to be singing.
- If you're shy (or tone-deaf), then go up in a group. You don't have to sing, because there won't be enough mikes, and the best, most confident singers will always hog them, anyway, so you can relax.

Help! I'm having a party and I want my house to look different.

This is easy to achieve and cheap, too.

• Move furniture out or to the sides to create a new atmosphere.
• Choose one color and go with it, e.g., white flowers, white balloons, white pillows or tablecloths draped over the chairs, glow-in-the-dark stars or tiny string lights draped everywhere. Gorgeous and easy.

Help! How can I tell if someone's lying?

It's all in the body language.

• Avoiding eye contact. If someone's lying, guilt often prevents them from being able to make and keep eye contact.

• Fidgeting. The human brain finds it difficult to lie, so it makes the liar twitchy. If someone's scratching their neck or fiddling with their shirt, it's possible they are lying — especially if they're avoiding eye contact, too!

• Slip-ups. People usually rehearse what they're going to say when they tell a lie. So if you're not convinced they're telling you the truth, listen to their story and then ask a question or pretend you didn't hear properly. If their story changes, you know they are telling lies.

Help! I always get bored during school vacations.

Don't just sit there, do something.

- Throw a DVD/video party.
- Make a compilation tape or CD of your favorite tunes.
- Jazz up your bedroom — put up a hammock, dye your sheets, or paint your walls.
- Have a picnic with your friends — if it's cold or raining, have it indoors.
- Make a mega ice-cream sundae.
- Pitch a tent in your yard or bedroom and camp out with a friend for the night.
- Go through your favorite photos and arrange them in a colorful photo album.
- Create your own magazine with articles, quizzes, cartoons, and drawings.
- Host a barbecue, even if you have to eat it indoors.
- Clean out your closet.

Help! I've spilled something on my favorite top. What do I do?

Take action right away.

- Makeup remover works on everything from coffee to chocolate. Squirt a little over the stain (test on a small invisible area first to be sure), leave for a few seconds, then dab with a damp cloth.

- For serious offenders like ketchup, you'll need to use special stain removers and detergents. Follow the instructions carefully.

- If you have nothing else on hand, use soap and water. But you should *not* use water on items labeled DRY CLEAN ONLY.

Help! I've let my friend down. How can I apologize?

When "I'm sorry" isn't enough, here are some tips for effective apologies.

- Regret the way you acted.
- Take responsibility for what you did.
- Take steps to make sure it doesn't happen again.
- Say "I'm sorry, I know I acted badly and I'll never do it again." And mean it!
- Keep it short, simple, and fairly serious.

Help! I don't know what to buy my dad for his birthday!

Here are three things to remember when buying your dad a present.

- Think about what he likes. Does your dad have a hobby or play a sport? Does he like music or reading? Do some detective work — he'll appreciate the effort.
- If you're still not inspired, ask your mom or aunt — any female adult who knows him well.
- If all else fails, he'll always appreciate socks. Don't believe me? Look at your dad's feet next time he takes his shoes off. I bet his socks are full of holes!

Help! I have to get braces soon. How can I stop people from looking at my mouth?

Stop worrying! Here are some things to remember.
• Wear your braces with confidence. They don't make you look ugly!
• Still not feeling confident? Treat yourself to a new haircut or get yourself a new top — anything to make you feel good.
• Don't stop smiling!
• People only notice change — after a while they won't notice your braces. They'll only think about it again when you have them taken off!

Help! I have no idea what I want to be when I grow up, and it's worrying me.

Don't panic. You've got years to decide. Here's a simple exercise to help.
• Write a list: The ten things I most want to do with my life. It could include anything from being the editor of your favorite magazine to swimming with dolphins.
• Now ask yourself: What am I doing to achieve these goals?
• Start taking small steps toward making your dreams reality. If you want to be the editor of a magazine, get involved in your school paper. If your school doesn't have one, start one. If you want to swim with dolphins, find out where you can see them in their natural habitat.
• Remind yourself of your dreams regularly and plan to take yourself one step further toward them.

155

'Bye

I really hope you've enjoyed reading this book as much as I enjoyed writing it. Remember, you have it in you to be whoever you want to be – Keep believing in yourself and it will happen. You have lots to look forward to, and getting there is half the fun!

Take care of yourself.

'Bye for now!
Sarah xx

P.S. If you liked **Pink Pages**, please tell all your friends about it. Thanks!
I appreciate it.

INDEX

PINK PAGES

Notes

Notes